COOKING, BLOKES + ARTICHOKES

A MODERN MAN'S KITCHEN HANDBOOK

BRENDAN COLLINS

FOREWORD BY CURTIS STONE
PHOTOGRAPHY BY JEAN CAZALS

KYLE BOOKS

COOKING, BLOKES + ARTICHOKES

BRENDAN COLLINS is executive chef of Birch, Larry's and The Corner Door in Los Angeles. He has appeared on Spike TV's *Bar Rescue* and MTV's *House of Food*, as well as The Esquire Channel's *Knife Fight*. He currently lives in Los Angeles with Eden, his wife, and Saffron, his daughter.

Drawing on his training in butchery and belief in using the whole animal, Collins is dedicated to using only the best ingredients and cooking food that he likes to eat. He worked at several prominent restaurants in London, including those of Marco Pierre White, before moving to L.A. He combines impeccable French technique, seasonal California ingredients and his inimitable 'British lad' attitude to his cuisine.

CONTENTS

BRENDAN COLLINS: NO BULLSHIT BLOKE, NO BULLSHIT FOOD.

Bren and I met over 15 years ago whilst working the stoves at Marco Pierre White's revered restaurant Quo Vadis in Soho, London. We worked alongside each other for only a couple of years, however it was here that skill, technique, work ethic and a solid culinary foundation were drummed into us 17-hour day after 17-hour day – and here that the bromance was born.

Even if I wanted to, I can't seem to escape this bloke. Interestingly, we've both wound up as expat chefs navigating the restaurant scene in Los Angeles. Brendan gained more freedom to explore and define his personal cooking style here, and has earned immeasurable success and respect in our adopted city. While I bloody enjoy a feed at the restaurants he currently helms, Birch and Butcher's Dog, I'm lucky enough to be a frequent face in his home, too. And that means I'm on the receiving end of his simple and hyper-seasonal 'California ingredients meets impeccable French technique meets British lad' home-cooked food. Yum!

There's no doubting that my mate knows his way around an animal and ensures everything from a pig's head to a lamb's belly tastes utterly succulent and moreish. Pulitzer Prize-winning food writer for the *LA Times*, Jonathan Gold, says Collins 'is at heart a big meat guy', which is absolutely fair game, however don't be skipping over his vinaigrettes, pickles and condiments and 'Veg' and 'Pudding' chapters.

Every recipe has rallied for its place on these pages. I know because I've been there on the family and friends nights, tasting his restaurant plates prior to the doors officially opening and it was no different with his first book. (By the way, first book! Awesome achievement mate!!!) Someone had to make sure his brioche doughnuts packed just the right balance of butter, bourbon and sweetness, and that the potatoes cooked three-ways were equally delicious when mashed, boiled or turned into triple-cooked chips – those chips are devilishly good stuff! I'm an absolute sucker for paella, I love Spanish food and have spent quite a bit of time there – Bren's Quinoa and Shellfish Paella takes me right back to the shores of Valencia, the birthplace of paella, whilst simultaneously reminding me that his 10+ year tenure in Southern California has had its way with him, too.

Beyond his Brit lad, pub loving, 'meat man' exterior, Brendan is really a big softie and is forever encouraging of his mates in the industry. I love that in this book, he gets a chance to share his knowledge, experiences and passion with a bigger audience now (to you, ya smart cookies who have bought this book!) and he'll no doubt inspire you to cook anything from a classic Lemon Tart to a Duck and Walnut Terrine. I'd go as far as to say, this is one of those extra special cookbooks you want to read and cook your way through from cover to cover. Do this and I know you'll gain newfound confidence and competence in the kitchen and you'll add some truly impressive dishes to your repertoire. Plus (and this is the best bit), you'll be eating some downright delicious food and bringing plenty of happiness to the special people in your life.

Bren, you're a cheeky bastard mate, but I love ya! Wishing you all the success in the world with *Cooking, Blokes + Artichokes*. It's a winner.

CHEERS ALL,
Curtis

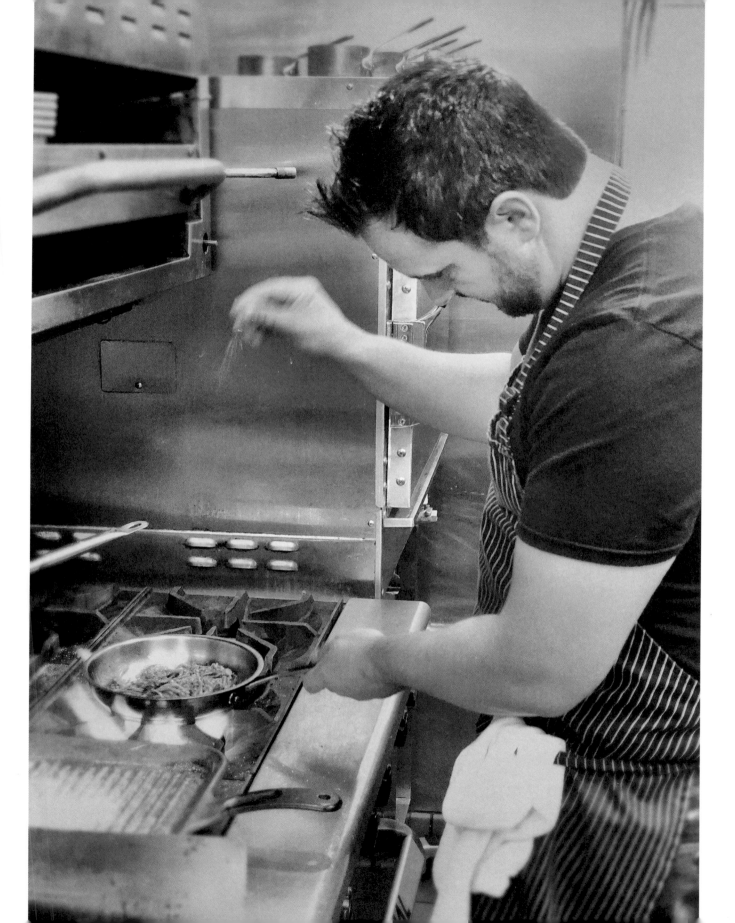

INTRODUCTION

MY VIEWS ON FOOD ARE QUITE SIMPLE: it should be fresh, tasty, and no more complicated than it needs to be. That isn't some kind of 'ethos' dreamed up over days spent gazing philosophically at a bunch of radishes. It's the only thing that makes sense to a bloke raised above pubs in the north of England.

When I was young, my parents worked as pub relief managers; when the owners went away on holiday, my folks would step in, take over shop and run the business temporarily. Moving through England from pub to pub, I learned a lot about life and something about cooking. There's no real equivalent to England's country pubs in the United States. In little towns and along rural byways all across the nation, they function as coffee shop, bed and breakfast and restaurant – not to mention post office, town hall, senior centre, confessional and communal living room.

The way that some kids love to take apart stereos or build model airplanes, I always gravitated to the kitchens with their hissing pans and warm smells.

This was before anybody used the word *gastropub*, when the food you found in rural pubs was pretty much universally unaffected, homely fare. But there was good cooking and bad cooking, and even at the age of ten I knew the difference between the two. Some pubs ran Sizzler-style operations, slinging freezer-burned burger patties and tinned vegetables, just a notch above fast food. Others took a real interest in local ingredients and from-scratch preparations. I remember one kitchen helmed by a legit old cruise liner chef making his own *jus* and

hollandaise sauce, serving local game meats and whatever fresh vegetables he could get his hands on, in some middle-of-nowhere village. That was, and still is, my idea of how good food ought to be.

After my parents split up, I went to live with my grandparents, and it was there that I had my first true education in eating with the seasons. My granddad approached food with the thrift and self-sufficiency of a man who lived through the war and, worse, postwar rationing. He had his greenhouse and a little orchard at the top of the garden, and from that we had tomatoes, cucumbers and courgettes in summertime, apples and pears and carrots and turnips in winter. He raised pigeons and chickens and we ate them too.

Becoming a chef was quite a natural transition. At the age of fifteen, I left school, left home and never looked back. I enrolled in cooking school; I got my degree on a Thursday and by Sunday was on a train to London looking for work. I was seventeen. That was the beginning of a restaurant career that has taken me through the kitchens at Le Gavroche, Quo Vadis, Mélisse – some of the best and swankiest restaurants in London and Los Angeles. I've cooked some pretty fancy food over the years, but the country cooking of my boyhood has always remained at the front of my mind. I've never lost sight of what a good, honest homemade dinner looks like.

I find that food has become too complicated for my tastes these days. Restaurant dishes tend towards the experimental, heady and, frankly, weird. Dinner has turned into an opportunity for a chef to test the bounds of his own creativity and invention, and the ingredients sometimes feel more like a dare than a proper meal: dehydrated scallop chips, fermented grasshopper paste, foraged lichen. If you ask me, it's a distraction from the real purpose of a restaurant, which is to feed people well. Leave them full and happy. And more than ever, the way we chefs cook in restaurants influences the way people cook at home.

Flip through today's food magazines and cookery books and what you find is restaurant food – dishes designed to be cooked inside the confines of a professional kitchen that don't make a whole lot of sense in the home. Restaurant kitchens, with their battalions of hot-footed cooks, dedicated dishwashing staff, walk-in refrigerators, industrial venting systems, high-end ingredient suppliers and hundreds of paying customers, are set up for cooking food with lots of pieces and steps. Home kitchens, built to feed families, are not. If I spent my days off trying to cook the food that I make at Birch in my home kitchen – that pokey little room with a square metre of counter space and burners that barely get hot, by restaurant standards – I'd have nothing but headaches. Home cooking and restaurant cooking are simply two different beasts, and a cookery book made up of restaurant dishes only discourages anybody picking up a knife to learn.

This is not a book about my restaurant, Birch. It's not a commentary on contemporary Los Angeles dining, or an ode to British gastropubs or a food memoir about what it feels like to be a chef. It's simply a collection of lessons and recipes designed to work properly, taste delicious and help you get a good meal in front of your family.

I'm sharing what I've learned in twenty-three years at the cooker about feeding people well and enjoying yourself in the process. The recipes run the gamut from simple snacks to holiday feasts; from my formula for making a proper vinaigrette to a foolproof technique for braising meat. My aim throughout is to impart a set of broader kitchen skills that will turn you, little by little, into the kind of confident, intuitive cook who can cruise a supermarket aisle with purpose, and knows what to do with a fridge full of food just by rummaging through it.

This is the cookbook that I'd hand to any of my mates looking for tasty, no bullshit food that's going to be better than whatever he can warm up from the freezer or order for takeaway. Sometimes it's about a quick meal, thrown together on the fly – mushrooms on toast or a lamb burger charred up nicely on the grill. But when you have some time to tinker, I'll show you how to roast a pig's head to glistening, golden perfection, cure your own duck prosciutto and put up jars of a silky, savoury caramelised onion compote that you can slather on pretty much anything for a crazy flavour boost. Over time, you'll grow into a solid, intuitive cook – just wait and see. So go ahead; roll up your sleeves and let's get cooking.

A SHANDY WHILE YOU COOK

Most people who meet my missus are quite jealous when they hear that her husband is a chef. They must think that I come home from a seventy-hour workweek, pull on the old apron, and start boiling stocks, cracking lobsters, harvesting the home garden and milking the dairy cow that we keep tied up out back.

The truth is that by the time my day off rolls around, I'm usually knackered and want nothing more than to enjoy my limited time with my family, eating good but simple food and having a laugh together. Whether or not you cook for a living, I can imagine that the feeling is the same. Work is hard. Feeding your family ought to be easy.

Home cooking and restaurant cooking couldn't be more different. At the restaurant we're under tremendous pressure, with ten to fifteen cooks working flat-out to produce dishes that will be memorable and worthy of the considerable investment it takes these days to dine out. Needless to say, sipping on a cocktail while you work is out of the question.

At home, it's a different story. My only goal is to make something fresh and wholesome for the people I love, without taking myself too seriously in the process. On these occasions, there is no better beverage than the shandy. Half lager, half lemonade, the shandy is a family drink: mellow, refreshing and light enough on the alcohol that it won't put this tired chef immediately to sleep.

SERVES 1

300ml lemonade (my favourite is R. White's)

300ml of your favourite beer (pilsners work best)

1. Pour the lemonade into a 600ml glass and stir with a spoon to release some of the carbonation.

2. Pour the beer on top.

3. Drink quickly, then repeat steps 1 and 2.

THE KITCHEN TOOLKIT

THE RECIPES IN THIS BOOK USE VERY LITTLE IN THE WAY OF SPECIALITY EQUIPMENT, and that's intentional: I'd rather you invest in good-quality basics than stuff your kitchen full of every last strawberry huller, fondue kit, bread machine, panini press and electric pepper mill.

Below is an accounting of everything you need to make all the recipes in this book, listed roughly in order of importance. For the pricier items, like stainless steel or copper cookware, I highly recommend having a look through TK Maxx, outlet shops and the internet. You can often find products from reputable brands like Cuisinart, All-Clad and Calphalon there at incredible prices.

KNIVES: You're not going to get very far in the kitchen without a knife. Chefs tend to keep a kit of very expensive Japanese or German numbers, but those require frequent skilled sharpening, which is a lot for a home cook to take on. Your essential blade will be a 20–22cm chef's knife, and for that I recommend one of the inexpensive ones made by Victorinox. Get a little hand sharpener and use it frequently to keep the blade in good working order, and simply replace it for around £25 if it becomes too dull to work with. The same goes for your paring knife, a 7.5–10cm blade for small cutting and peeling jobs. You should also have a serrated knife about 20cm in length, good for breads and any task where you'll be sawing through a tough exterior. Those don't require sharpening, so feel free to spend a bit more. A serrated paring knife comes in handy too. That covers the essentials, but there are lots of speciality knives you can buy if interested, such as a boning knife, filleting knife, petty knife, cleaver and slicer.

CHOPPING BOARDS: These should always be wooden, large enough so that bits of things aren't constantly falling off the sides, but not too large to easily position on your counter. Sharp knives get stuck in plastic boards and form grooves where bacteria settles. Glass chopping boards are the worst, dulling your knives and making a terrible sound when you work on them. Never, ever.

MIXING BOWLS: Preferably made from stainless steel, because it's light, durable, and easy to clean.

KITCHEN SCALES: In Europe, our recipes tend to call for ingredients by weight, so a good kitchen scale is absolutely essential. Go with a digital scale, which will be the most accurate and easiest to use.

MEASURING SPOONS: Stainless steel is ideal.

METAL SPATULA: For flipping items in a pan or on the grill.

RUBBER SPATULA: For thoroughly scraping out bowls and pans and stirring scrambled eggs in a non-stick frying pan.

WOODEN SPOON: For stirring anything on the hob. Don't put these through the dishwasher, or the wood will dry and crack.

WHISK: For, well, whisking.

TONGS: The tool of choice for retrieving pasta from boiling water, turning sturdy meats and vegetables in a barbecue or pan and several other kitchen tasks. Choose a basic stainless steel version.

TEA TOWELS: Get a good stock of cotton towels and use them as you would oven mitts, as well as for cleaning surfaces, covering dough while it rises, drying salad greens and the like. Put them through the laundry frequently.

BAKING SHEETS: It's a good idea to have a couple with rimmed edges and a couple without. Aluminium ones are fine.

GREASEPROOF PAPER, CLINGFILM, TIN FOIL: Always have a roll of each on hand, and don't buy the cheap stuff.

FINE-MESH SIEVE: For straining liquids. One that's 18–20cm in diameter is ideal. If possible, get one with a double layer of mesh for finer straining.

COLANDER: For draining pasta and washing vegetables, including lettuce for salad. Don't buy a salad spinner! What a waste of space.

MICROPLANE GRATER: For zesting citrus and grating cheese, garlic, chocolate, ginger and so on.

DUTCH OVEN/CASSEROLE: A heavy, enamelled cast-iron pan will probably get more use than any other piece of cookware. Get one of 4.7–5.7 litre capacity. I like Lodge, which is half the price of the Le Creuset brand and just as good.

CAST-IRON PAN: These are naturally non-stick and hang on to heat well for powerful searing. A good diameter is 30cm, and Lodge is the brand of choice.

SAUCEPANS: Get a small, medium and large saucepan, plus a big stockpot. Ideally they should be made from triple-ply stainless steel. All-Clad is what we use.

ROASTING TIN: Invest in a large one, because it's always better to have slightly too much room in the pan than not enough. Splurge on a stainless steel one, or even copper, for food to cook most evenly.

BLACK STEEL FRYING PAN: This is the tool of choice for pan-roasting fish. A good diameter is 23cm.

NON-STICK FRYING PAN: I know that Teflon is out of vogue because of toxicity issues, but a non-stick pan of some sort is really ideal for omelettes, crepes, pancakes and even fish. Calphalon makes good ones. Wipe them out with kitchen paper after use and don't scrub or scrape them, which damages the surface.

COPPER SAUTÉ PAN: Copper is expensive, but it distributes heat very evenly and heats quickly. If you buy just one copper pan, make it a 4–5 litre high-sided sauté pan. It can be used for practically any hob job, from sautéing vegetables to searing meat to making sauces.

GRILL PAN: Similar to the cast-iron pan except with ridges, if you want to achieve grill marks indoors.

FOOD PROCESSOR: This machine makes quick work of chopping and dough making; in a pinch it can be used for puréeing too, although it doesn't typically achieve results that are as smooth as what a good blender can do. Choose one with at least a 2-litre capacity. Cuisinart and Kenwood are good brands.

BLENDER: For making ultra-smooth sauces and soups (plus smoothies and margaritas). Vitamix is the brand of choice in professional kitchens; they are expensive, but can blend virtually anything as smooth as a baby's bottom.

STAND MIXER: Not only very useful in mixing doughs, but can be used with various attachments for making pasta, mincing meat and more. KitchenAid and Breville are my favourite brands.

PRESSURE COOKER: Today's digital countertop models are worlds better than the old hob battleaxes I'm used to. There are many good brands with all sorts of bells and whistles, so buy according to your budget.

MEAT THERMOMETER: I prefer digital versions, because analogue ones need to be calibrated before each use, which is a pain. We use a brand called Taylor.

SUGAR THERMOMETER: Whereas a meat thermometer gives an instant temperature read, sugar thermometers read temperature continuously. They are necessary for gauging oil temperature whenever you're deep-frying.

BARBECUE: Gas and charcoal are both fine; get whatever your taste and budget allows for.

PESTLE AND MORTAR: For grinding spices. These are typically made of granite or marble and the heavier, the better. Keep in mind that they're meant to be used in a smooth grinding motion; if you bang them together, they will break or chip (if you drop them on your toe, God help you!).

LOAF TINS MEASURING ABOUT 21 × 12 × 11cm: Also known as 1-pound loaf tins. These are used for making breads or smaller terrines. There are very good non-stick versions now that don't require you to grease the tin before use, and those are the ones to buy.

FLAN TIN: Buy one that's extra deep, 23cm in diameter, and made of non-stick steel rather than glass or earthenware.

PEPPER GRINDER: Peppercorns should always be ground fresh, never bought pre-ground, because their flavour dulls quickly. Buy a grinder that allows you to adjust the size of the grind.

FISH SLICE: This speciality spatula has a razor-thin leading edge designed for getting underneath fish skin in a pan and keeping the whole fillet in one piece as you turn it. It's very helpful when pan-roasting a skin-on piece of fish.

SPIDER: This is a skimming tool made from mesh, and it's the best choice for removing items from the fryer. Oil clings too heavily to a slotted spoon and will drip everywhere. Spiders can also be used to fish objects out of boiling water.

ROLLING PIN: Always wooden. I've used an empty wine bottle in a pinch, but a rolling pin is better.

PASTA MACHINE: The best choice is a pasta attachment for your stand mixer, which extrudes the dough and sheets and cuts it into the desired shapes. You can also get a hand-crank model made by Imperia. Those are cool and old school but take forever.

TERRINE DISH: This heavy earthenware or metal containers are good exclusively for making terrines such as the Smoked Salmon and Potato Terrine (page 84) and Duck and Walnut Terrine (page 97). A loaf tin works if you don't want to invest in one.

PASTRY BAGS AND METAL TIPS: A pack of large disposable bags and a few plain round tips, for piping fillings into things like Fried Courgette Flowers (page 68) and Sriracha Devilled Eggs (page 61).

MEAT MINCER ATTACHMENT: This connects to your stand mixer and is necessary for the Duck and Walnut Terrine (page 97).

ICE CREAM MACHINE: Some sort of ice cream apparatus is essential if you want to make Eggnog Ice Cream (page 169). Options range from basic manual devices that you stir by hand to fully automatic ones with their own condensers, so that no pre-chilling of bowl is necessary. Choose whatever's right for your level of ice cream enthusiasm. Don't spent hundreds of pounds on a machine you're going to use twice.

FRYER: A countertop fryer isn't a necessity, but it takes the guesswork (and much of the risk and mess) out of deep-frying. Breville makes a nice model.

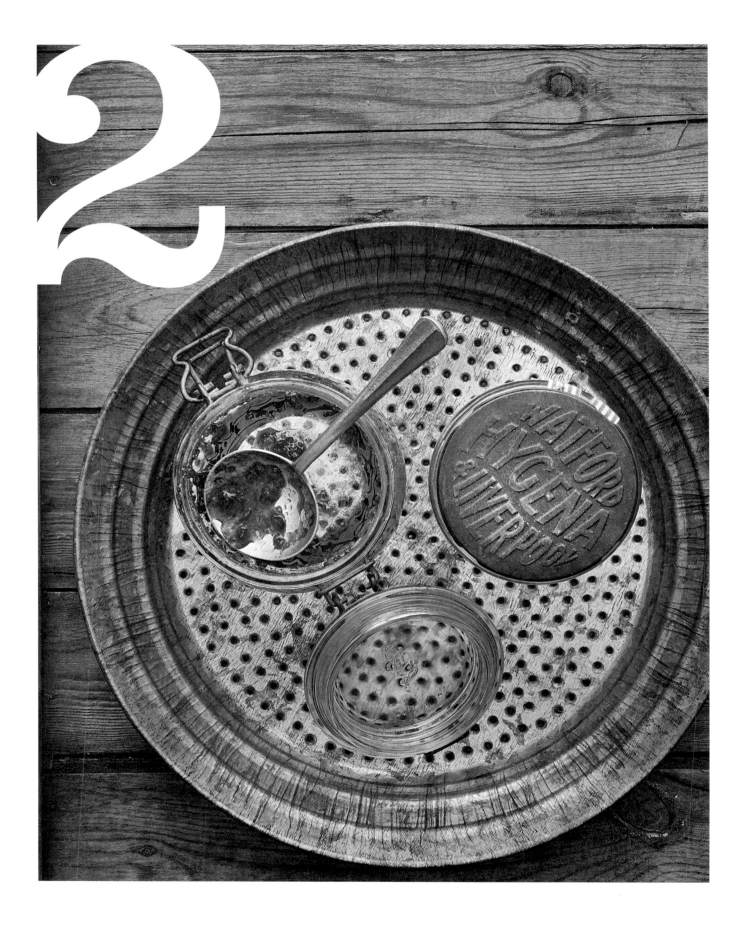

THE OTHER TOOLKIT

LIFESAVER FLAVOURS

MOST COOKERY BOOKS HIDE THE CONDIMENT RECIPES IN THE BACK, LUMPED IN with all the sauces and stocks that you can pretty much guarantee nobody will ever use. That's a bloody shame, because it's my opinion that great condiments – pickles, preserves, vinegars, oils and the like – are the flavour boosters that mean the difference between a mediocre plate and a spectacular one. Experienced cooks know that a fillet of fresh striped bass with a lovely knob of homemade lemon butter can knock your socks off harder than a meal that takes hours to make, filled with all kinds of fancy footwork. Stock your fridge with a few killer homemade condiments, which can be made in batches and kept for weeks or even months and the cooking is already halfway done.

Before you get all pumped up with DIY spirit, keep in mind that not everything is worth the effort to make from scratch. The recipes in this chapter focus your effort only where it's going to pay off big-style. For instance, mayonnaise is best left to the good people at Hellmann's/Best Foods, who make a product that's probably better than anything you're going to whip up from eggs and oil in your own kitchen. Same goes for Dijon-style mustard. Let Grey Poupon or Maille do the work for you.

PICKLED MUSTARD SEEDS

These are a nice alternative to spreadable mustard. You get that spicy, tart mustard flavour plus a little crunchy texture as the seeds pop in your mouth. Use them on sandwiches or add a big spoonful to a charcuterie board or cheese plate. They'll keep in the fridge for six months minimum, so don't worry about whether you'll make it through the whole batch. By the way: the term *pickle* simply means to preserve something in vinegar or brine, the latter of which is a solution made from salt and water.

MAKES 720ML

145g yellow mustard seeds

240ml white wine vinegar, preferably Chardonnay

180ml mirin

100g granulated sugar

1 tablespoon coarse sea salt

1. Take a small saucepan and add the mustard seeds plus enough cold water to cover them, then place it over a high heat. Once the water has reached a boil, remove the pan from the heat and strain the mustard seeds through a fine sieve. Repeat this process, known as *blanching*, twice more, using fresh cold water each time.

2. Place the blanched mustard seeds, vinegar, mirin, sugar and salt with 180ml water in a small saucepan and bring the mixture to the simmer over a low heat. Cook uncovered until the seeds are plump and tender, about 1 hour. If too much liquid evaporates, add just enough water to cover the seeds.

3. Remove the seeds from the heat, cool them to room temperature and store them in a clean jar in the refrigerator.

CARAMELISED ONION COMPOTE

Onion compote is one of the most perfect things there is in life. This is no exaggeration. It's got salt, sweetness from the onions and brown sugar, sourness from the vinegar, *umami* that develops during the long, slow cooking process and bitterness from that little bit of charring that's inevitable whenever you're cooking onions in a pan.

It can be used both hot and cold. It can be made with little effort and keeps for two weeks. And it works on practically anything: on sandwiches, with steak, in salads, on a charcuterie board, inside an omelette, on top of a hot dog. It's perfect alongside a piece of grilled swordfish. You can chop it up and add it to tuna tartare. I've even puréed it and added it to sauces.

Below is my basic onion compote recipe; you can customise it depending on the use. If you're going to do it with roast beef, add a little horseradish. Spoon in some Dijon mustard if you plan to serve it with pork, or add a little wasabi to customise it for salmon. If you want a little more texture, add mustard seeds. You can always add soy sauce along with the vinegar to make it really savoury. With the addition of beef stock, you've got a base for French onion soup. See what I'm talking about? It's the world's best condiment.

MAKES 240ML

120ml extra virgin olive oil

900g white onions, thinly sliced

1 tablespoon brown sugar

½ bottle stout or porter beer

2 tablespoons beef stock

1 tablespoon balsamic vinegar

coarse sea salt and freshly cracked pepper

1. Heat the oil in a large, heavy-based saucepan set over a medium-high heat until it shimmers. Tip in the onions and brown sugar, stir to coat them with oil and spread them evenly in the pan. Reduce to medium-low and cook, stirring occasionally, until you smell the sugars release and the onions become soft and translucent, 30–45 minutes.

2. Chuck in all the liquids and cook until they're three quarters reduced, continuing to stir the onions regularly – or else they'll burn and taste like shit. Season the mixture with a good grind of pepper and a teaspoon or two of salt, to taste. Remove the onions from the heat and let them cool completely.

3. Load the onions into a sterilised jar and close it tightly. The compote will keep in the fridge for around 2 weeks . . . if it lasts that long.

PRESERVED LEMONS

The hardest thing about this recipe is the patience it takes to wait thirty days for the incredible cured lemon skins that turn up at the end. Since I'm not known for my patience, I make a big batch once a month so that I never run out.

What's so great about preserved lemons? The salt-sugar rub really mellows them, pulling out all the bitterness and leaving just bright, sunny lemon flavour. If you're wondering how to use them, the better question is how can't you use them. Chop up the skin and toss it into stews or grain salads, blend it into salad dressings and sprinkle it on fish or chicken for starters.

MAKES 6 PRESERVED LEMONS

6 Meyer lemons
100g coarse sea salt
100g granulated sugar
4 bay leaves
240ml fresh lemon juice

1. Gently scrub the lemons under cold water. Using a sharp paring knife, score each lemon 6 times down the length of the fruit, cutting deep into the flesh but keeping the lemons intact.

2. Mix together the salt and sugar. Snip the bay leaved with a pair of scissors and this to the mixture. Squeeze each lemon gently to open up your incisions, then rub the salt-sugar mixture into the fruit liberally.

3. Press the lemons into two sterilised 240ml mason jars, cover with lemon juice and close them up tight.

4. Refrigerate for at least 30 days (and up to 6 months). To use, slip the skin off the lemon flesh and slice it as needed. You can give the skin a quick rinse if you want, but I like to use them with a bit of the nice salt rub on them. Don't try to use the lemon flesh, though, as that is really punishingly salty.

SPICY PICKLES

Most shop-bought pickles are loaded with artificial colours, industrial-grade salts and surfactants. (What's a surfactant? Yeah, exactly.) So right there, the pickles you make yourself are going to be way better than something you buy at the supermarket. Don't shove them to the back of the fridge and forget about them, though: although technically pickles don't really go bad, they're at their freshest, crispest and most delicious for only about a month (same goes for bought pickles). Aside from the traditional cucumber version, you can also use this pickling liquid to preserve cauliflower, beetroot, carrots – any veg that's sturdy enough to sit in liquid for a long while.

MAKES 3 × 600ML JARS

480ml warm water

420ml distilled white vinegar

2 dried chipotle chillies

100g granulated sugar

8 garlic cloves, sliced

1½ tablespoons coarse sea salt

1½ teaspoons celery seeds

½ teaspoon chilli flakes

12 American-style pickling cucumbers, such as Kirby

1. Combine the water, vinegar, chillies, sugar, garlic, salt, celery seeds and chilli flakes in a large bowl. Stir and let stand at room temperature for 2 hours, or until the sugar and salt are dissolved.

2. Divide the cucumbers among three 600ml sterilised wide-mouth mason jars. Cover them with the pickling liquid.

3. Close the jars tightly and refrigerate them for at least 10 days and up to 1 month.

HERBY PICKLES

As if you need another reason to love pickles: they happen to be really good for you. Vinegar aids digestion by keeping yeast levels in check in your gut, improves blood sugar levels and keeps your metabolism up. A pickle a day keeps the doctor away!

MAKES 4 LITRES

1.8kg American-style pickling cucumbers, such as Kirby

100g coarse sea salt

2.4 litres white wine vinegar

1 teaspoon allspice berries

1 teaspoon cracked white peppercorns

1 teaspoon cracked black peppercorns

4 sprigs each dill, parsley, chervil, tarragon and basil

1 tablespoon demerara sugar

80g shallots, chopped

1. Split the cucumbers in half lengthways, sprinkle the cut surfaces evenly with half of the salt and let them sit for 30–45 minutes. This extracts water from the cucumbers and allows them to pickle more deeply.

2. In a large pan set over a high heat, combine the rest of the salt, the vinegar, allspice, peppercorns, herbs, sugar and shallots with 480ml water. Bring to the boil, then remove from the heat. Let the pickling liquid cool to room temperature, then refrigerate it until cold.

3. Divide the cucumbers among four sterilised 1-litre wide-mouth mason jars and cover them in pickling liquid. Seal them. Leave them in the fridge for about a week before digging in. They'll keep for up to 6 weeks.

SWEET CHILLI MARMALADE

This recipe is a secret weapon of mine, frankly a lazy fix for any dish that needs a quick shot in the arm. The combination of sweet, heat and salt is positively addictive. Use it anywhere you'd put hot sauce. So, pretty much everywhere.

MAKES 3 × 600ML JARS

12 red Fresno chillies, roughly chopped

one finger-size piece fresh ginger root, peeled and roughly chopped

8 garlic cloves, peeled

450g cherry tomatoes

600g light muscovado sugar

240ml red wine vinegar

1. Chuck the chillies (seeds and all), ginger and garlic into a food processor and pulse the stuff until it's very finely chopped.

2. Scrape the chilli mixture into a heavy-based pan with the tomatoes, muscovado sugar and vinegar. Bring to the boil over a medium-high heat, skimming off any scummy looking stuff that comes to the surface, then turn the heat down to a slow simmer. Cook uncovered for about 1 hour, stirring occasionally.

3. When the marmalade becomes sticky, continue cooking for 10–15 minutes further, stirring frequently so that it doesn't fucking burn – otherwise you've just wasted your time. It should now look like thick, bubbling lava.

4. Remove the pan from the heat and once it has cooled off slightly, pour it into sterilised mason jars. Close them up tightly while still hot, then leave them to cool completely. The jars should vacuum seal as they cool, allowing the marmalade to stay fresh for up to 3 months in a cool, dark cupboard. If the tops don't pucker down for any reason, store them in the refrigerator straightaway.

WALNUT MUSTARD

There was a period of six months there when I was on a total mustard craze. I was grinding my own mustard seed, experimenting with different styles and colours, tinkering with pickling techniques, working in different flavours and textures. In the end I only got two thoroughly enjoyable recipes out of the obsession, but that's how it goes with these things. They can't all be winners.

This recipe came about as an accompaniment for duck pâté. I wanted the pâté to be somewhat sweet, so the walnuts and vinegar were there for bitterness and acidity to balance the flavours. It turns out that walnut mustard is great not only with pâté but also on cheese plates and sandwiches, and I even stir it into a butter sauce for roast halibut or chicken.

MAKES 360ML

2 tablespoons walnuts

6 tablespoons
Dijon mustard

6 tablespoons
grainy mustard

60ml white wine vinegar,
preferably Chardonnay

sea salt and freshly
ground black pepper

4 tablespoons walnut oil

1. Preheat the oven to 160°C/gas mark 3.

2. Spread the walnuts in a single layer on a baking sheet. Toast them until golden and fragrant, about 5 minutes.

3. Place the walnuts in a pestle bowl and break them down with a mortar until the largest pieces are about the size of a cracked peanut. Add the Dijon mustard and continue mixing. Add the grainy mustard and vinegar, mixing still. Add a small amount of salt and pepper at this point.

4. Now slowly add the walnut oil in a fine drizzle while continuing to mix; the final product should have the texture of chunky peanut butter. Taste and add salt and pepper as desired.

ROMESCO SAUCE

This classic Spanish recipe is traditionally used as a dipping sauce for vegetables, but I think it's just too good to confine to one purpose. I sometimes smear it on top of a firm white fish such as halibut or sole before baking, or serve it alongside grilled meats. Romesco keeps for about a week in the fridge if you hold back the parsley and add that right before serving. And a word about seasoning: always taste food for salt at the same temperature you'll be eating it. Everything tastes saltier when hot, so it may need a dash more salt once cooled.

MAKES 480ML

4 large garlic cloves

150ml olive oil

1 (2.5cm) slice baguette

3 tablespoons almonds

3 tablespoons hazelnuts

2 medium shallots, sliced

½ teaspoon smoked paprika

115g piquillo peppers

6 tablespoons Tomato Confit (page 31)

1 teaspoon tomato purée

2 tablespoons red wine vinegar

2 tablespoons water

salt and freshly ground black pepper

2 tablespoons chopped fresh parsley

juice of ½ lemon

1. First, blanch the garlic: fill a small saucepan two thirds full with cold water and bring it to the boil. Toss in the garlic and cook for 2 minutes, then drain it in a colander or mesh sieve.

2. Add 2 tablespoons of the oil to a medium frying pan set over a medium heat. Fry the slice of baguette until golden brown all over, about 2 minutes on each side. Remove it from the pan.

3. Add the almonds and hazelnuts to the same pan and toast them until golden and fragrant, 2–3 minutes. Remove them from the pan and add another 2 tablespoons oil, followed by the shallots and garlic. Reduce the heat to medium-low and sweat the garlic and shallots, stirring them frequently; continue until they smell sweet and are completely translucent, 4–5 minutes. Add the paprika and cook for a further minute.

4. Stir in the piquillo peppers, Tomato Confit and tomato purée and cook for a further minute. Add the vinegar and scrape up any browned bits stuck to the pan (this is called *deglazing*). Add the toasted nuts and bread back to the pan and cook for 1 minute, stirring.

5. Dump the contents of the pan into a food processor and blend until smooth. With the food processor running, add the remaining 90ml oil in a steady stream, followed by the water. Taste it, and season it to your liking with salt and pepper. Transfer to a bowl and let cool.

6. Add the parsley and lemon juice and adjust the salt to taste.

TOMATO CONFIT

These roasted, oil-packed tomatoes are good for lots of uses: on sandwiches, mixed into risotto, as a condiment with steak or salmon – anywhere you want a really intense tomato flavour. The tomatoes and herbs infuse the oil too, which is delicious in its own right. Try tossing spaghetti with diced confit tomatoes and a bit of their oil in place of making a sauce.

Getting the peel off tomatoes can be a huge pain in the arse. The key here is straight-up selection. What you're looking for is bright green vines and stems, even colouring, no breaks in the skin, and a really fragrant herbal smell. The tomato should be red; not pink, not greenish, but red. It's always best to use local tomatoes when they're in season, but we're concentrating the flavour so much in this recipe that any ripe tomatoes will work.

MAKES 1 LITRE

1.35kg vine-ripe tomatoes

2 garlic cloves, thinly sliced

1 sprig rosemary

4–5 leaves fresh basil

240ml extra-virgin olive oil

sea salt

1. Fill a stockpot two thirds full with water and bring it to the boil over a high heat. Fill a large bowl with ice water.

2. Dig the eye out of the top of each tomato with a paring knife, then score a cross into the opposite end. Working 4 or 5 at a time, drop the tomatoes into the boiling water. Remove them after exactly 10 seconds using a slotted spoon and immediately transfer them to the ice water. Repeat until all the tomatoes are blanched. The peel should now separate easily from the tomato.

3. Remove the tomatoes from the ice water, discard the peel, and cut them in half (top to bottom, not through the middle).

4. Place the tomatoes cut-side down on a nonreactive baking sheet (aluminium, steel, copper or iron all make tomatoes taste metallic. If you have baking sheets made of any of these metals, which almost everyone does, line them with greaseproof paper to avoid this effect).

5. Preheat the oven to its lowest temperature, around 90–100°C/gas mark ¼.

6. Place a slice of garlic, a few rosemary needles and a small piece of torn basil on top of each tomato half, then drizzle with a touch of oil and sprinkle them with salt. Transfer the sheet to the oven and roast for 1 hour. Turn off the heat and leave them in the oven for a further hour, then remove them and cool to room temperature.

7. Carefully place the tomatoes and their juices in a 1-litre jar and cover them with the remaining oil; make sure they are fully submerged in oil to keep them from oxidising and going bad. Close the jar and refrigerate for 10–14 days.

PICKLED RED ONIONS

I've loved pickled onions ever since I was a kid. Down at the chip shop, there were jars of golf ball-size pickling onions soaked in malt vinegar; this is a traditional pairing with fish and chips, good for cutting through all that grease. And in the gastronomically remedial 1980s, a little piece of cheddar and a silver-skinned cocktail onion stuck through with a toothpick was a popular hors d'oeuvre. But if you weren't brought up on the flavour, English pickled onions can taste a bit harsh, as they're soaked in straight vinegar. My recipe incorporates sugar and spices to balance the flavour a bit and take the edge off. These are a great way introduce a little acid to sandwiches or salads.

MAKES 1.2 LITRES

900g red onions (3 medium or 2 large), thinly sliced

360ml white wine vinegar

100g granulated sugar

½ cinnamon stick

5 cloves

1 bay leaf

1 star anise

dash of chilli flakes

1. First, blanch the onions: fill a medium saucepan two thirds full with cold water and bring it to the boil. Toss in the red onions and cook for 2 minutes, then drain them in a colander or mesh sieve.

2. Meanwhile, in a separate saucepan, combine the vinegar, sugar, cinnamon stick, cloves, bay leaf, star anise and chilli flakes. Bring to the boil over a high heat, then reduce it to a simmer. Cover and simmer for 5 minutes. Add the blanched onions and simmer for a further minute.

3. Transfer the onions and liquid to a sterilised glass jar and cool to room temperature. Close them up tightly and store in the refrigerator for up to several weeks.

INFUSED OILS AND VINEGARS

One thing that oils and vinegars have in common is they're both great at taking up flavour and locking it in ready-to-deploy form. Infusing them with herbs, spices, fruit zests and so on is simple, and such a good way to add dimension to your cooking that it would be cruel not to include them in a book of this nature. Here are a few sample recipes, but I encourage you to raid the spice cupboard and produce aisle and do as your heart desires. Just remember not to heat olive oil above 48°C, because it burns easily and will develop an off flavour, and when infusing either oil or vinegar with soft ingredients such as fresh fruits, vegetables and herbs, too much heat will cause them to break apart and turn the liquid cloudy and unappealing.

CITRUS OIL
MAKES 600ML

1 teaspoon coriander seeds
480ml olive oil
peel of 1 lemon, pith removed
peel of 1 lime, pith removed
peel of 1 orange, pith removed

1. In a small saucepan over a medium heat, toast the coriander seeds until golden, fragrant and starting to pop. Reduce the heat to medium-low, add the oil and gently bring the temperature to 48°C (about the temperature of bathwater).

2. Add the citrus peels and pour the mixture into a bottle or jar. Allow it to steep at room temperature for 2 hours; use immediately or keep refrigerated for up to a month.

SPICY HERB AND GARLIC OIL
MAKES 600ML

480ml olive oil
4 garlic cloves, smashed and peeled
4 whole dried chillies, such as árbol or bird's eye
2 sprigs each thyme, rosemary and tarragon
2 fresh sage leaves

1. In a small saucepan over a medium-low heat, combine the oil, garlic, chillies and herbs and gently bring the oil temperature to 48°C (about the temperature of bathwater).

2. Pour the mixture into a bottle or jar. Allow it to steep at room temperature for 2 hours; use immediately or keep refrigerated for up to 1 month.

(continued)

CHILLI VINEGAR

MAKES 1 LITRE

1 litre rice wine vinegar
1 fresh habanero chilli
1 fresh jalapeño chilli
1 dried chipotle chilli
2 shallots, thinly sliced
1 small bunch of coriander

1. Place all the ingredients in a clean 1-litre mason jar and close the lid tightly.

2. Fill a stockpot two thirds full with water and bring it to the boil. Using a pair of kitchen tongs, place the jar into the water carefully and continue to boil for 1 hour. Remove the jar and let it cool. The vinegar will stay good for months; just a heads up: it will continue to generate heat and flavour from the chillies as it ages.

BLACKBERRY-ANISE VINEGAR

MAKES 1 LITRE

1 litre red wine vinegar
260g blackberries
3 star anise
3 sprigs of tarragon

1. Place all the ingredients in a clean 1-litre mason jar and close the lid tightly.

2. Fill a stockpot two thirds full with water and bring it to the boil. Using a pair of kitchen tongs, place the jar into the water carefully and continue to boil for 1 hour. Remove the jar and allow it to infuse for 24 hours at room temperature, then remove the star anise. After about a week, this vinegar is stunning both in flavour and colour. The vinegar will stay good for months; when using it, avoid the solid ingredients and use the liquid only.

HERB BUTTER

Compound butters – aka butter mixed with tasty bits – are dead easy to make, and they are a simple way to add a quick hit of flavour to meats, fish, vegetables and so on. I've always got at least a couple of different versions knocking about in my freezer, where they keep for months. This simple herb butter is a tasty basic example, but you can flavour butter with pretty much anything you want (any sort of herb or spice, sugars, cheeses, chillies – you name it), so let your imagination run wild.

MAKES 500G BUTTER

500g unsalted butter, preferably Kerrygold or Lurpak (don't buy the cheap stuff; you get what you pay for)

3 tablespoons fresh lemon juice, from about 2 lemons

2 garlic cloves, very finely chopped to a fine paste with a Microplane

2 heaped tablespoons finely chopped fresh flat-leaf parsley

sea salt and freshly ground black pepper

1. Allow the butter to soften. If you're too disorganised to take it out of the fridge an hour or so before you need it, then cut it into small chunks and chuck it in the microwave for 5 seconds at a time until soft. Be careful not to let it melt, because you can't un-melt butter.

2. In a large bowl using a plastic spatula, beat the butter vigorously for a minute or two until it reaches a creamy, cake icing-like texture. This is pretty hard work, kind of a chef's version of going at a boxing speed bag. It helps to think of somebody you don't like.

3. Add the lemon juice, garlic and parsley and continue to beat the butter until the ingredients are fully mixed. Season with salt and pepper.

4. Spread out a square of clingfilm at least 30cm long across your work surface, then scoop the mixed butter onto the plastic. Roll the butter into a cylinder inside the clingfilm. Tie the ends of the clingfilm into knots so that you have an enclosed, sausage-like cylinder of butter. Chill or freeze until needed. Slice off disks of butter for use on the table or in cooking, being sure to reseal the butter well before returning it to the fridge or freezer.

THINGS ON BREAD

MAN FOOD IN A PINCH

LEGEND HAS IT THAT SANDWICHES ORIGINATED IN BRITAIN IN THE EIGHTEENTH century, the brainchild of John Montagu, Earl of Sandwich. As a result, the sandwich has been called Britain's biggest contribution to gastronomy. I only wish we could rightfully claim this culinary masterwork, which I would personally rank above the steam engine, telephone and lightbulb in the scheme of British inventions. But the reality is, the idea of putting things between bread – whether or not you call it a sandwich – is ancient and universal, from the *bánh mì* of Vietnam to France's *croque-monsieur*, Malaysia's *roti* and Greece's *gyros*.

Men have a particular affinity for sandwiches, and I think that's because we're not shy about eating with our hands and letting things dribble down our chins. The almighty sandwich is one of the first foods I learned to love. After twenty-five years of working my arse off in kitchens, I can now cook myself virtually anything, but sandwiches remain a pillar of my home cooking repertoire. I love them for their utter simplicity and range: a sandwich makes sense at any time of day, from a bacon and egg number at breakfast to the grilled cheese you fire up as a late-night snack. Once you understand the basics of putting flavours and textures together, you can feed yourself well in almost any situation. This chapter will teach you how.

MUSHROOMS ON TOAST

Whether for breakfast, lunch, or a late-night snack, this open-faced sandwich is a real melting pot of flavours, one of those dishes with a good meaty feeling to it but little actual meat. All kinds of mushrooms work; if it's springtime and you can get your hands on porcinis or chanterelles, they're really the cream of the crop. But readily available options like oysters, shiitakes, portobellos and creminis will do just fine.

When you get mushrooms home from the shop, keep them in the refrigerator between kitchen paper or in a brown paper bag. Most mushrooms that you buy are cultivated, not picked wild, so you don't even need to wash them before use. If there's any visible dirt, wipe it off with a damp towel. You really want to avoid submerging them in water, as mushrooms are like sponges and will soak up any liquid you put them in.

SERVES 2 (IF YOU'RE HUNGRY) OR 4 (FOR A SNACK)

4 slices sourdough bread, just shy of 2.5cm thick

1 tablespoon olive oil

4 slices prosciutto

2 tablespoons soy sauce

2 tablespoons yuzu juice or lemon juice

¼ teaspoon wasabi paste

1½ teaspoons toasted sesame oil

55g unsalted butter, plus a knob for frying the eggs

4 large organic eggs

350g mixed wild mushrooms

1 garlic clove, crushed

2 tablespoons sliced spring onions, white and pale green parts only

a handful of fresh parsley leaves, finely chopped

sea salt and freshly ground black pepper

1. Toast the bread, cut each slice in half, and set them aside. Heat a large frying pan over a medium-high heat and add the oil. Once the oil is hot, add the prosciutto and fry until golden and crisp, about 2 minutes per side. Break the crisp ham into large pieces and set it aside on kitchen paper.

2. In a small bowl, whisk together the soy sauce, yuzu, wasabi and sesame oil.

3. In a separate frying pan, melt the knob of butter over a medium heat. Add the eggs and fry until they're as well-cooked as you like them (I like the whites just opaque and the yolks super runny). Remove them from the pan to a plate and set them aside.

4. Turn the heat up to medium-high and add the remaining 55g butter. Let the butter cook until nut brown and beginning to smoke, then add the mushrooms. Leave them alone for at least a minute – that's how they'll get a nice deep, meaty sear – then give them a stir and cook for a further minute. Add the garlic and spring onions and continue to cook for 3–5 minutes.

5. Add the soy-yuzu dressing and cook until the liquid is reduced to a glossy, viscous sauce. Stir in half of the parsley, taste the mixture, and add more salt if necessary and some pepper. Pile the mushrooms high on the toasts and top them with the prosciutto, fried eggs and more fresh parsley.

THE PERFECT SANDWICH, EVERY TIME

I've included a few sandwich recipes in this chapter to give you the blueprints for some of my favourite combinations. To tell you the truth, though, relying on recipes for sandwiches is kind of like reading your half of a conversation from a script. Sandwiches are almost always best when you gin them up on the fly, adapting to whatever ingredients you find yourself faced with.

First of all, you can't make a great sandwich out of shitty ingredients. It's just not possible. You can't build a Porsche out of old Ford parts. So – not to sound like a complete prat – but let the ingredients speak to you. What looks the best in the supermarket, farmers' market, bodega, convenience shop or wherever else you're shopping? Really fresh cucumbers, salt and mayonnaise on toast is going to make for a better lunch than a ham and cheese sandwich if all you can find is slimy, pre-packaged meats and processed cheese.

Resist the urge to overdo it. You want to be able to taste each ingredient in the sandwich, rather than slathering on a bunch of random relishes and spreads and setting up a flavour death match. Less is more. To me the perfect sandwich is a *jambon beurre*, the French classic made from really good crusty baguette, a thin layer of ham, and high-quality butter. It's just three ingredients, and it couldn't be better.

Balancing textures is also important. If you're using a hard rustic bread, for instance, you've got to make sure that everything inside is easy to chew. Add something really sturdy like roast beef and you'll burn out your jaw. On the flipside, a combination like egg salad on white bread is going to make you feel like you're eating lunch in an old folks' home. You've also got to think about the way the whole thing swallows. If you've got a lot of dry textures together – crusty bread, chicken breast, cheddar, for example – you'll end up drinking water to get a bite down, which really kills the flavour.

Remember practicalities too. You want to be able to eat the thing without detaching your jaw, so don't make it ten centimetres thick. And there is nothing worse than biting into a sandwich and having it fall apart in your hands. Make sure the bread can stand up to your fillings.

Lastly, if you make a sandwich in advance, the best thing to wrap it in is greaseproof paper. Avoid foil and clingfilm, because the sandwich will get nasty and soggy if it can't breathe. Don't put any wet ingredients – washed lettuce, condiments, tomatoes – directly against the bread, or in a matter of an hour or two the bread will go to shit.

GRILLED SKIRT STEAK AND HORSERADISH SANDWICH

Skirt steak is the ideal sandwich cut. It's cheap, fast and easy to cook, tender enough that you won't put your jaw out trying to bite through it and it has a rich, intense flavour of beef to it. It's also a naturally slim piece of meat, no more than 1.25cm thick and about ten centimetres wide, which makes it the perfect dimensions for laying a slab between two slices of bread. Adding the heat of horseradish, creamy mayo and peppery rocket rounds out the flavours perfectly. If you think you like roast beef sandwiches made with gray deli roast beef, just wait. You'll go nuts for this.

SERVES 2

350g skirt steak

120ml Skirt Steak Marinade (recipe follows)

coarse sea salt

2 slices ciabatta bread, about 15 × 10cm, sliced down the middle

30g unsalted butter, softened

75g mayonnaise

1½ tablespoons horseradish (or more, to suit your taste)

2 handfuls of rocket

freshly ground black pepper

1. Trim any excess fat off the steak, rub it with the marinade, and place it in a ziplock bag or covered container in the refrigerator for at least 2, but no more than 8 hours; more than that and the meat will turn mushy when it cooks.

2. Fire up the barbecue and let it get hot, or place a grill pan or cast-iron pan over a high heat for 5 minutes. Remove the steak from the marinade, scrape off any excess herbs and garlic, season it liberally with salt, then grill the meat to your liking. Medium-rare will take about 1 minute per side.

3. Toast the bread if you want, or simply butter the bloody stuff. In a small bowl, mix together the mayonnaise and horseradish to your desired spiciness.

4. Build up your sandwich by slathering the horseradish mayo on the bottom slice of bread, then put down a bed of rocket, followed by your meat, a seasoning of black pepper and the top slice of bread.

SKIRT STEAK MARINADE
MAKES ABOUT 120ML

120ml olive oil

1 tablespoon chopped garlic

1 tablespoon chopped fresh thyme

1 tablespoon chopped fresh parsley

1 tablespoon chopped fresh rosemary

2 tablespoons Sprite or 7-Up (the phosphoric acid will tenderise the meat to melt in the mouth)

zest of ½ lemon

Dump all the ingredients in a blender and blend until combined.

STILTON AND ONION MARMALADE GRILLED CHEESE

Stilton is not exactly your classic grilling cheese, but it's one of our proudest British cheeses and it's funky and terrific paired with rich, buttery brioche. Give it a chance!

Let's talk grilled cheese basics, because no matter what kind of cheese or bread you use, the procedure is going to be the same. The biggest mistake people make with grilled cheese is getting the pan too hot, which means the bread burns before everything inside turns warm and gooey. Keep the heat low and slow. Along the same lines, if you get greedy and pile the cheese on too heavily, it won't melt through; 3–6mm in thickness is ideal. When it comes to bread, the softer the better, and don't use anything with bits of whole grain, nuts, or fruits, all of which will burn. Always spread the outside of the bread with soft butter, which is key to achieving that crisp, golden exterior.

SERVES 1

30g unsalted butter, softened

2 (2cm thick) slices of brioche

5 tablespoons Caramelised Onion Compote (page 21)

70g sliced Stilton or other creamy, not crumbly, blue cheese

1. Lightly butter both sides of both slices of bread; the bread and cheese both have a lot of fat in them already, so don't go too crazy.

2. Spread the inside of both slices of bread with the onion compote and place the cheese evenly in the middle.

3. Heat a black steel, Teflon or cast-iron pan – something the bread won't stick to – over a medium-low heat. Cook the sandwich until the bread is golden brown and the cheese begins to turn soft and warm, 3–4 minutes, then flip it and repeat on the other side. Slice in half and eat immediately.

OPEN-FACED PORK LOIN SANDWICH WITH BUTTERHEAD LETTUCE

I know there's something a bit dainty and foofoo about the idea of an open-faced sandwich, but even though I really enjoy bread – everything about it, from weighing the ingredients to kneading it, shaping it, baking it, smelling it, and most of all eating the stuff – it does have a nasty tendency to fill you up. Removing one slice from the sandwich equation can improve your bread-to-meat ratio, bringing all the ingredients back into balance. Try this one on for size and see what you think. It's a great recipe to scale up and make for a whole army of people: buy a 1–1.4kg pork loin and roast it, get a couple loaves of great bread, and lay all the ingredients out in serve-yourself fashion.

SERVES 2

170g center-cut pork loin

Pork Brine (recipe follows)

2 big slices of hearty bread, such as baguette or sourdough

30g unsalted butter, softened

½ recipe Butterhead Lettuce Salad (page 121)

2 Herby Pickles (page 25)

1. In a ziplock bag or covered container, combine the pork and brine and let it sit in the refrigerator for at least 2 but ideally 4 hours. Give the pork a quick wash and dry it with kitchen paper.

2. Preheat the oven to 190°C/gas mark 5.

3. Place the pork in a small metal or glass tin and roast it until the internal temperature of the meat reaches 57°C, around 10 minutes (20 minutes per 450g is a good guideline for pork, in case you're cooking a bigger piece of meat). Remove the meat from the oven and let it rest for 10 minutes.

4. Toast the bread if you like, then butter it generously. Slice the pork as thinly as possible. Top the bread with a thick layer of pork, top that with the Butterhead Lettuce Salad, and serve with a pickle on the side.

PORK BRINE
MAKES 480ML

480ml water

1 tablespoon salt

1½ teaspoons granulated sugar

1 sprig coriander

1 clove

1 star anise

Combine all the ingredients in a small saucepan and bring to the boil over a high heat. Remove the pan from the heat and cool to room temperature.

CIABATTA

No matter what the artisan bread-baking books have told you, a lot of breads just aren't that easy to make well at home. Take baguettes, for instance, or those big, round, crusty French *pains de campagne:* you really need a special steam-injection oven for those to turn out right. Ciabatta is a different story. It does just fine in any oven. It's supposed to look rustic, so you can do an ugly job of shaping the loaves without feeling like you've screwed it up. Plus it's a top-notch sandwich bread, soft enough to chew easily but sturdy enough to stand up to fillings. Like any bread, it's best eaten the same day – remember, we're not adding any preservatives here – but wrapped tightly in foil, it'll be OK the day after you bake it, too. Especially toasted.

MAKES 2 LOAVES

FOR THE MOTHER

⅛ teaspoon dried
active yeast

2 tablespoons warm
(40–46°C) water

75ml room-
temperature water

130g strong bread flour,
preferably organic

FOR THE BREAD

½ teaspoon dried
active yeast

2 tablespoons warm
(40–46°C) whole milk

150ml room-
temperature water

1 tablespoon olive oil,
plus more for greasing

260g strong bread flour,
preferably organic

1½ teaspoons sea salt

1. First, make the mother: in a small bowl, stir together the yeast and warm water and let sit for 5 minutes, or until it's milky and frothy. Dump this yeast slurry into a larger bowl with the room-temperature water and flour and stir the mixture until it forms a smooth paste (no flour lumps!), maybe 4 minutes. Cover the bowl with clingfilm and leave it in a cool room for at least 12 hours. It should triple in size at least. You can keep a mother for years and she'll continue to generate flavour — you just have to keep feeding her (sparked your curiosity, have I? Check out page 50 for more information).

2. Now, make the bread: In a small bowl, stir together the yeast and warm milk and let it sit for 5 minutes, or until it's slightly frothy. In a stand mixer fitted with the dough hook, combine this yeast slurry, a fistful of the mother (that'll be a cup or so), the water, oil and flour and mix it at low speed until the flour is just moistened. Beat the dough at medium speed for 3 minutes. Add the salt and beat the dough for a further 4 minutes. Scrape the dough into a large oiled bowl and cover it tightly with clingfilm. Let the dough rise at room temperature until it doubles in bulk, about 1½ hours. At this point, God willing, the dough will be sticky and full of air bubbles.

3. Ready two rimless baking sheets by covering them with well-floured sheets of greaseproof paper. Turn the dough out onto a floured work surface and cut it in half. Remove each half to its own baking sheet. Working gently, lads, and trying not to knock too much air out of the dough, form the dough into rectangles about 23 × 10cm; handle the dough as little as possible and don't worry if the loaf shapes are uneven. Just call them 'rustic'. Dimple the loaves with floured fingers and dust the tops with flour. Cover the loaves with dampened kitchen paper and let them rise at room temperature until almost doubled in bulk, 1 hour 30 minutes–2 hours.

4. Meanwhile, preheat the oven to 220°C/gas mark 7.

5. Bake the ciabatta loaves for 20 minutes, or until pale golden. Using a large spatula, transfer them to a rack to cool. Eat them the same day, or freeze them wrapped in foil inside a ziplock bag.

A WORD TO YOUR MOTHER

Call it a mother, a sponge, *pâte fermentée*, pre-ferment, or fermentation starter: if you want to make bread with seriously good flavour, the best way to do it is to add some dough that's been sitting around your kitchen for a while. And I mean a long while.

When you combine water, flour and yeast, the yeast feeds on the flour, converting the carbs to acids and alcohols with a whole range of lovely flavours. That's fermentation. Keep giving the yeast flour and water and the fermentation will continue indefinitely, layering flavour on top of flavour. Now you have your 'mother'. There are people who literally pass these things down across generations.

You've got to feed the mother every couple of days to keep it alive, so it's not unlike having a pet – that means if you go away on vacation for the week, you're either going to have to give it to a friend to look after or pop it in the fridge and take your chances. Every 2–3 days, remove a quarter of the dough (either use it to bake bread, or just throw it away if you must) and add fresh flour and water. So, if the dough is stored in a litre-size container, you'll remove 250ml of dough, mix together 65g flour and 120g water and add that in. If you want to make a sourdough, leave some pineapple juice or grapefruit juice out until it goes off and add that instead of water.

Store the mother in a warm, dark place in a jar or plastic container large enough for it to triple in size and wrap it in clingfilm poked through with holes so that it can breathe. Think of it as your own personal flavour factory, churning away in your larder.

BRIOCHE

Brioche is kind of like a bread that wants to be a pastry. The dough is rich, soft and buttery and caramelises really nicely when baked. As a sandwich bread, it's amazing with smoked fish and meat. I also love it in grilled cheese with sharp, cheddary cheeses that balance out its richness.

Brioche is traditionally baked in special round tins, but those are really expensive, so back when I was working in London we came up with a cheapskate workaround: we baked the loaves in the big 2.5 litre tins that restaurants get things like tomato juice and tinned fruit delivered in. It's pretty hard for a home cook to get his hands on tins that large, but if you can find them, I highly recommend giving the method a try.

MAKES 2 LOAVES

520g unbleached plain flour

65g granulated sugar

4 ½ teaspoons dried active yeast

2 teaspoons sea salt

6 medium eggs, at room temperature

120ml whole milk, at room temperature

225g unsalted butter, cut into 16 pieces, softened, plus more for buttering the tins

1 medium egg yolk

1. Dust off your stand mixer and fit it with the paddle attachment. Mix the flour, sugar, yeast and salt on low speed to combine them. Add 4 of the eggs and the milk and continue mixing on low speed. Once the dough shows signs of coming together, swap out the paddle for a dough hook.

2. Mix the dough on medium speed for a couple of minutes, then scrape down the bowl and the dough hook. Mix for a further couple of minutes, or until the dough starts to look elastic, then scrape down the bowl and hook again.

3. With the mixer on medium-low speed, start adding the butter a few pieces at a time. Once all of the butter has been added, increase the speed to medium and mix for 3–4 minutes. Then – you guessed it! – scrape down the dough hook and bowl one more time. We're trying to make sure this dough is as evenly combined as possible. Now mix the dough again until it's smooth and shiny, 4–5 minutes. The dough will slap against the sides of the bowl to announce that it's ready.

4. Place the dough on a baking sheet, cover it with clingfilm, and refrigerate for at least 2 hours and up to 24 hours. If the dough had a lengthy refrigeration time, you'll want to let it warm to room temperature before proceeding, about 2 hours. Meanwhile, butter two 21 × 11cm loaf tins (these are also known as 1-pound or loaf tins).

5. Turn the dough out, top down, onto a clean, lightly floured work surface. Form the dough into a neat ball by folding the sides toward the middle. Divide it into 2 equal pieces; they should be 535g each, if you're keeping score. Drop them into the loaf tins and cover them with clingfilm (at this stage, the brioches can be wrapped well and frozen for up to a month). Let the dough rise at room temperature until almost doubled in size, about 1½ hours. It should spring back when gently poked with a finger.

(continued)

6. Meanwhile, position an oven rack in the centre of the oven and preheat it to 190°C/gas mark 5.

7. In a small bowl, make an egg wash by beating the remaining 2 eggs and 1 egg yolk. Lightly brush the tops of the brioches without letting the egg wash drip down into the tins, which can make the loaves stick to their tins. Bake until dark golden brown on top and golden on the sides (you can lift the brioche slightly to peek in at the edge of the mould), about 18 minutes. For those who like thermometers, the internal temperature should be 88°C. Let the brioches cool on a wire rack for 10 minutes before unmoulding. Eat immediately, or cool, wrap airtight and freeze for up to a month.

HOW TO BUY BREAD

I've given you recipes for ciabatta and brioche, and I do hope you'll make them at least once if only to see what it's like. But I'm a realist. I know that week in, week out, most blokes will be buying their sandwich bread, not making it. That's perfectly fine, as long as you're smart about it.

First of all, do not visit the supermarket aisle with those pre-sliced, plastic-wrapped, undead zombie loaves. They're full of preservatives and added gluten and God knows what that doesn't belong in bread. Bread isn't meant to stay soft for days or even weeks on end. It's unnatural. Always go the freshly baked route if you can. Some supermarket bakeries are now producing very good breads.

How can you tell if you're dealing with good bread? The crust is the most important thing – it should be firm and springy. Good bread has some heft to it. If it feels hollow, then it's full of air and cheap fillers. Smell it; bread should always have a good strong whiff of yeast, which is how you know it's made with real yeast and not artificial, industrial 'super proofers'.

Recently there's been a big resurgence in small bakeries where you can get truly excellent loaves at a good price, while supporting a small business at the same time. Best case scenario is a local bakery that's using organic or imported flour. Not to get too political, but I really believe that all the weed killers and pesticides being sprayed on the wheat grown in the UK may well be what's making it hard for many of us to stomach bread (so then, not the gluten after all). In my house, we've gone fully organic with our bread and we're all feeling a lot healthier for it.

The reality is that fresh bread – real bread, made from flour, yeast, water, salt and nothing else – has a very short shelf life. It just does. Don't expect it to last more than 24–48 hours from the time it leaves the oven. The good news is that it freezes very well, which allows you to buy 3 or 4 loaves at a time without sacrificing quality or throwing a bunch away. As soon as you get home, immediately slice what you won't eat the same day and freeze it in a ziplock bag. Now you can take slices out of the freezer on demand. And bread straight from the freezer makes the absolute best toast: crispy on the outside, tender on the inside.

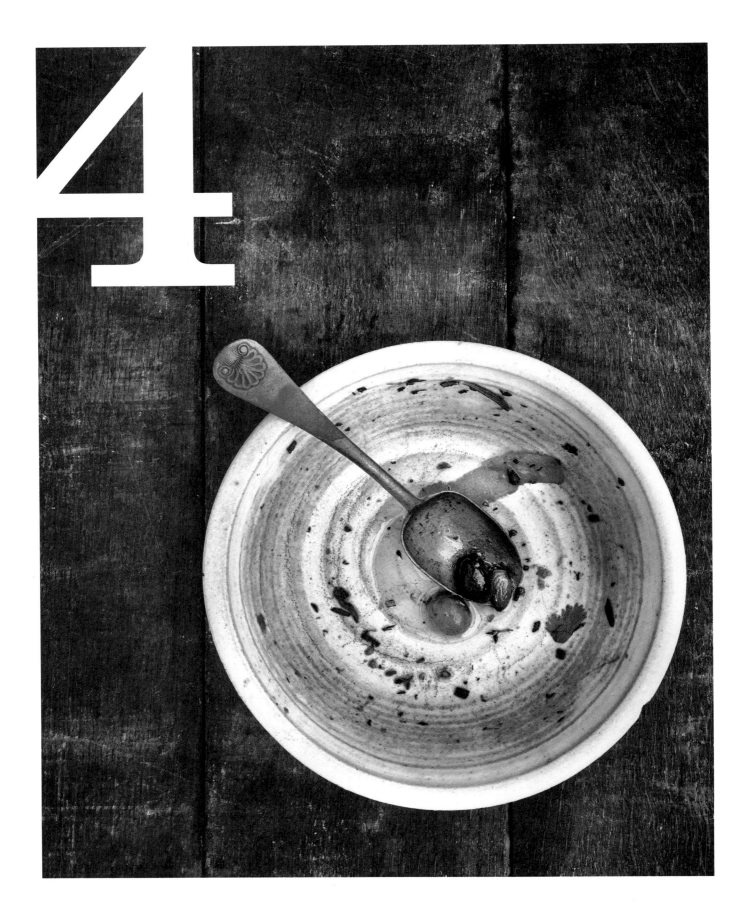

THE CHIPS ARE DOWN

THERE'S NOTHING GLOOMIER THAN SITTING DOWN AT THE END OF A LONG DAY TO A tatty bag of pretzels or crisps. That's why I've put together this selection of tasty, easy-to-execute snacks that will come in handy whether it's just you and the missus, a few mates over for beers, or you're hosting a full-on dinner party. Time to toss out your old faithful Cheesy Wotsits, beef jerky and energy bars, roll up your sleeves and make something worth eating.

I hear it said all the time that snacking is bad for you. Snacking isn't bad for you; it's what we choose to snack on most of the time that turns us soft around the middle: the cheap shit that's full of preservatives, artificial additives and loads of sugar. You'll notice the recipes in this chapter ain't exactly rabbit food – we're talking devilled eggs, *chicharrónes*, whipped lardo – but when you've made something with your own two hands, you know exactly what's in it. That's the absolute best way to look after your health. Everything doesn't always need to be mega-organic either, just as long as you use good, fresh, minimally processed ingredients. That's what this chapter is all about.

WARM MARINATED OLIVES

Great olives, ripened to perfection, cleaned of all their bitterness, and lovingly cured are now readily available at grocery shops – and not just fancy grocery shops either, but everyday supermarkets. You can put your own flavour stamp on them with this quick marinade. They'll keep absolutely forever in the fridge, and can be warmed in a matter of a few minutes for a no-hassle nibble.

MAKES 600ML

4 tablespoons olive oil (preferably Italian, for its spiciness)

3 tablespoons Caramelised Onion Compote (page 21)

peel of ½ lemon, pith removed

peel of ½ lime, pith removed

peel of ½ orange, pith removed

35g smoked almonds

30g Fresno or other mild red chillies, sliced as thinly as possible

1 sprig each rosemary, thyme, and savory (if you can find it; sage if not), finely chopped

450g of your favourite mixed olives (such as kalamata, picholine or castelvetrano)

1. In a medium saucepan heat the oil over a low heat to 35°C. It should feel about body temperature, but use a thermometer to check it if possible.

2. Add the caramelised onion compote, citrus peels, smoked almonds, chillies and herbs. Remove the oil from the heat and let the ingredients steep for 20 minutes. Add the olives and reheat it to 35°C. Strain off the oil and serve the olives warm. They can also be stored in the oil in the fridge for months.

SPICED ROASTED NUTS

When we were kids, my mum used to buy nuts still in the shell and give us a bowl and a cracker while we watched VHS tapes in front of the telly. The payoff was never rewarding enough for the amount of effort required to get the bloody things out, so I spent most of my teens and twenties resenting nuts. But when I became the executive chef at a hotel called Palihouse in West Hollywood, the owners asked me to come up with snacks to put out in bowls at the bar. I wanted to do something sweet and salty, because every chef knows that's what makes people keep drinking; nuts were the obvious choice. Using my homemade spice mix set ours apart from the sort of thing you could buy in a shop. The result was good enough that it cured me of my nut aversion. Now these are a staple at my house for every barbecue and Premier League football game.

MAKES ABOUT 450G

1 teaspoon chilli powder

1 teaspoon paprika

1 teaspoon garam masala

70g icing sugar

2 tablespoons coarse sea salt

60g shelled pistachios

65g shelled hazelnuts

50g shelled walnuts

60g cashews

65g shelled peanuts

65g macadamia nuts

1. Preheat the oven to 160°C/gas mark 3.

2. In a small bowl, mix up the chilli powder, paprika, garam masala, icing sugar and salt. In a large bowl, mix all the nuts.

3. Dust the spice mix over the nuts and mix it up with your hands until things are evenly distributed. Spread the nuts in a single layer on a baking sheet and bake them for 20 minutes. Serve them once they've cooled. They keep for about a week in an airtight container.

WHIPPED LARDO

The word *lardo* gives the distinct impression of something that's going to give you an early heart attack, but the truth is that animal fats, when obtained from quality sources, aren't nearly as bad for us as we've made them out to be in recent years. My granddad lived until he was well into his nineties, and he subsisted on the likes of butter, lard, cheese, full-fat milk and cream. So go ahead and enjoy your lardo as a tremendously tasty substitute for butter.

MAKES ABOUT 350G

225g top-quality pork back fat

100g coarse sea salt

1 garlic clove

1 teaspoon sherry vinegar

½ teaspoon coarse sea salt

½ teaspoon freshly ground black pepper

½ teaspoon finely chopped fresh rosemary

½ teaspoon finely chopped fresh thyme

warm crusty bread, to serve

thinly shaved radishes, to serve (optional)

handful of watercress, to serve (optional)

1. Sprinkle the pork fat with the coarse sea salt and place it in a container in the fridge for 24 hours. This is a simple cure, meant to pull out excess water and amplify the fat's porky flavour.

2. Wash the pork fat under cold water for 2 minutes, then cut it into 1cm pieces.

3. Grate the garlic using a Microplane grater; alternatively, smash it, sprinkle it with coarse sea salt and grind it to a paste using the back of your chef's knife. The latter method has the disadvantage of taking longer and making your chopping board smell permanently of garlic.

4. Chuck the pork fat, garlic, vinegar, ½ teaspoon coarse sea salt, pepper, rosemary and thyme into a food processor. Pulse the motor a few times to combine the ingredients, then process until smooth. Serve the lardo at room temperature with warm crusty bread and some shaved radish and/or watercress.

SRIRACHA DEVILLED EGGS

Who doesn't love a devilled egg? These one-bite beauties are the perfect companions to a cold beer – better than your mum's, although don't tell her I said so. Bet you can't eat just six!

A word about the eggs: don't be a cheapskate. Buy the free-range organic eggs. Not only is it the right thing to do, but you'll be rewarded by the better-tasting yolks of chickens who aren't being tortured.

SERVES 4–6

12 medium organic eggs

180g mayonnaise

½ teaspoon Thai red curry paste

zest and juice of 1 lime

drizzle of Sriracha sauce, plus more to taste

drizzle of Tabasco sauce

1 teaspoon Thai fish sauce

1 teaspoon Dijon mustard

sea salt

8 rashers crisp bacon, each broken into 3 even pieces

10g chopped fresh chives or green spring onion tops

1. Place the eggs in a large pan and fill it with warm water so the eggs are covered by 2.5cm. Bring the water to the boil over a high heat and boil the eggs for 8 minutes – it's best to set a timer so that you don't end up with overcooked, powdery egg yolks. Transfer the eggs to a bowl of ice water to chill down.

2. Peel the eggs, gently cut them in half from top to bottom, and remove the yolks to the bowl of a food processor. Add the mayo, curry paste, lime zest and juice, Sriracha, Tabasco, fish sauce and mustard and blend until smooth, about 1 minute (this can also be done by hand, but the yolks won't be as creamy).

3. Taste the yolk mixture and add salt if needed. If it's not devilish enough for you, add some more Sriracha.

4. Scoop the yolk mixture into a piping bag and squeeze it into the cavity of each egg white. Pro tip: if you don't have a piping bag, you can cut the corner off a ziplock bag, seal the yolk mixture inside, and squeeze it out that way.

5. Poke a piece of bacon into each egg half and sprinkle with the chives or spring onion tops. Pop open a beer and eat.

FRESH RICOTTA WITH CRUSTY BREAD

The first time you make this and don't fuck it up you'll be mighty impressed with yourself, and you're going to want all your mates around to see. But the truth is that making ricotta is dead easy, just as long as you get good-quality milk and don't scorch it by letting it get too hot. The straining process takes a little time, but you can put it aside and forget about it for half an hour.

MAKES 500G

1.5 litres organic whole milk

360ml organic heavy cream

coarse sea salt

1 tablespoon fresh lemon juice

2½ tablespoons distilled white vinegar

1 loaf crusty bread, such as a baguette

sea salt and freshly cracked black pepper

a little olive oil

1. Line a large sieve or strainer of some description with two layers of cheesecloth (or a coffee filter, in a pinch) and set it over a large, deep bowl.

2. Bring the milk, cream and 1 teaspoon coarse sea salt to the simmer in a large stainless steel pan (don't use one made from a reactive metal like aluminium or copper, which will make the ricotta taste funny) over a medium heat, stirring it occasionally. Add the lemon juice and vinegar and cook, stirring, until the mixture curdles, about 1 minute.

3. Pour the mixture into the prepared sieve and let it drain, discarding the liquid (called whey) from the bowl as necessary, for at least 15 minutes and up to 30 minutes. The longer it drains, the thicker the cheese.

4. Toast the bread; sprinkle the soft ricotta with sea salt and freshly cracked black pepper, drizzle it with a good slick of olive oil, and serve warm.

PORK SCRATCHINGS

When I was a kid, pork scratchings – also known as pork rinds, or *chicharrónes* to the Spaniards – were something I often had when I went to the pub with my parents. A shandy and a packet of pork scratchings. Since then they've found their way into mainstream gourmet kitchens, where they're valued for their intensely crunchy texture and the funky look they have about them. Mostly I'm just crazy for the way they taste. You're unlikely to find pork skin at the supermarket, but a local butcher should be more than happy to offload his excess to you for a few pence a pound.

SERVES 8–10

the skin from 1 pork belly (about 30 × 50cm), trimmed of excess fat and nipples, if present

coarse sea salt

sunflower or vegetable oil for frying

sea salt and freshly ground white pepper for seasoning

apple sauce or salsa for dipping

1. In a large pan, cover the pork skin by 5cm of water as salty as seawater. Weight the pork skin down with a plate to keep it submerged and bring the water to the boil. Boil, uncovered, until the water is white and the skin is soft and pliable but not falling apart, 1 hour 30 minutes–2 hours. Add more water as needed to keep the skin submerged; no need to watch it like a hawk the entire time, just check it from time to time to make sure the water doesn't boil dry.

2. Set a wire rack on top of a baking sheet and, using a slotted spoon, carefully remove the pork skin to the rack in an even layer. Chuck it in the fridge, uncovered, and allow it to chill for at least an hour.

3. Preheat the oven to its lowest temperature setting – this should be 80–100°C/gas mark ¼, depending on your oven.

4. Once the skin is chilled, use a spoon or a dough scraper (or even a wallpaper scraper) to remove all the fat; you have to be somewhat careful here not to break the skin.

5. Line a baking sheet with greaseproof paper and place the skin in a single layer on top. Dry the skin in the oven until all the moisture has evaporated and it becomes brown and brittle. This should take about 6 hours, but start checking it after 4. If it's gone black, you know you fucked up and you had better call the butcher and get some more.

6. Snap the skin into small pieces about 2.5cm square. I've used a Dremel in the past to create exactly uniform squares; I've also just snapped them with my fingers into uneven shapes. Either way works. At this stage, you can store the pieces in an airtight container in the cupboard for a couple of days before frying.

7. Take a heavy-based pan, like a Dutch oven, and fill it half full with oil. Position a thermometer in the oil and heat it nice and slow over a medium heat until the temperature reads between 195 and 200°C. It's important that the

temperature stays within this range. Fry a couple of pieces of pork skin at a time, prodding them until they puff up and turn crispy, about 15 seconds. Remove them to a kitchen paper-lined tray and season them with salt and pepper while still hot. Repeat with the remaining pieces. Serve immediately with applesauce or salsa, or cool them to room temperature and store them in an airtight container for up to 2 weeks.

BAGNA CAUDA WITH MARKET VEGETABLES

I grew up eating good but simple English food, so when I moved to London and was exposed to the diversity of cuisines there, my taste buds went into shock. I remember so well my first Caesar salad – exotic fare for a kid from Nottingham – and how surprised I was to discover that the gloriously rich dressing got its meaty flavour from anchovies. As it turns out, those nasty-looking little fillets are at the heart of many great dressings and sauces, including this one.

Bagna cauda simply means 'hot dip' in Italian, and it's a creamy, mildly fishy, fondue-like sauce that pairs particularly well with fresh vegetables. Needless to say, it will be a major upgrade from that seven-layer dip you've been serving since university.

SERVES 6

150ml extra virgin olive oil

4–5 garlic cloves, peeled and grated on a Microplane

12 anchovies preserved in olive oil, drained and finely chopped

4 tablespoons whole milk

85–115g unsalted butter, cut into chunks

various raw farmers' market vegetables, such as fennel, cauliflower, chicory, sweet peppers and courgettes

1. In a small saucepan over a low heat, combine the oil, garlic and anchovies and whisk them constantly for 3–4 minutes. The anchovies will break apart and disperse in the oil. Whisk in the milk, followed by 85g cold butter. As soon as the butter has melted, remove the sauce from the heat and give it a few more turns with your whisk so that everything is creamy and emulsified.

2. Taste the dip; if it's a bit too fishy for you, add another 30g butter. Just remember that you'll be eating it in small amounts to liven up plain vegetables, so it should have a powerful flavour.

3. Wash the veg and chop them into pieces appropriate for dipping. Serve with the warm dip.

FRIED COURGETTE FLOWERS

I love spring and summer, and it's not because I pull out the Bermuda shorts and SPF 100 and hit the beach. I'm always at work. It's because of the quality and freshness of the fruit and veg at the farmers' market. In the spring you have peas, morels, asparagus – everything green – and then through the summer all the colours: stone fruits, berries, peppers, aubergines, sweetcorn and tomatoes. Nestled in between all that are courgette flowers, which are the deliciously edible flowers of courgette plants. You'll find them at farmers' markets from May to September. Some chefs like to fill and steam them, but for me, the best way is fried crispy in beer batter, oozing with hot goat's cheese and dipped in chilli marmalade.

SERVES 4–6

225g creamy goat's cheese

4 tablespoons grated Parmesan

1 medium egg yolk

1 teaspoon chopped fresh basil

pinch of freshly grated nutmeg (less is more here)

pinch of cayenne pepper (ditto)

coarse sea salt and freshly ground black pepper

12 large courgette flowers

480ml tepid light beer

1 teaspoon dried active yeast

4 tablespoons vodka

115g sauce flour, plus more for dredging

2 medium egg whites

4–5 ice cubes

sunflower or vegetable oil for frying

Sweet Chilli Marmalade, for dipping (page 26)

1. In a small bowl, mix together the goat's cheese, Parmesan, egg yolk, basil, nutmeg, cayenne and a bit of salt and pepper and stir until smooth. Spoon the filling into a heavy-duty 1-litre plastic bag, squeeze out the air and seal it. Snip one of the corners off the bag to create a small hole. Gently insert the cut corner all the way to the bottom of a courgette flower and pipe about a tablespoon of the goat cheese filling inside. Twist the top of the flower closed, making sure to completely seal in the filling so that it won't tumble out. Repeat with the remaining courgette flowers and bang them in the fridge until the cheese is set, at least 30 minutes.

2. In a really large bowl, combine the beer, yeast and vodka, then whisk in the flour until smooth. Whisk the egg whites to soft peaks in a separate bowl, then gently fold them into the beer mixture. Drop in the ice cubes and let it sit covered with a tea towel somewhere warm until doubled or tripled in size, about 20 minutes.

3. Now we're going to make a deep-fryer. If you've got an electric one by chance, use it, because they're way safer; if not, take a heavy pan like a Dutch oven and fill it half full with cooking oil. Position a thermometer in the oil and heat it nice and slow over a medium heat until the temperature reads 180°C. Drop a bit of batter carefully into the oil; it should sizzle immediately. This setup will work for anything you want to deep-fry, not just courgette flowers.

4. Remove the flowers from the fridge and dredge them in flour on all sides. Shake off the excess flour and dip them into the beer batter. Let the excess batter drip off.

5. Gently lay the courgette flowers in the hot oil. Don't just lob them in, lads; I can't stress how stupid and dangerous that would be, as you don't want to be putting out a grease fire, ever. Working with about 6 flowers at a time, fry them until pale golden brown, 2–3 minutes. Use a metal spoon to flip them over from time to time so that they cook evenly. Remove them from the oil with a slotted spoon and let them cool off slightly. Serve them with sweet chilli marmalade for dipping.

GOUGÈRES

These fancy little cheese puffs are the original 'once you pop, you just can't stop' finger food. By some kind of Frenchie magic, they pack tons of toasted cheese flavour into a light, airy little ball. Gougères can be a bit tricky to make, so read the recipe all the way through before you start.

MAKES 15–20

120ml whole milk

115g unsalted butter, cut into small cubes

large pinch of coarse sea salt

130g plain flour

4 medium eggs

100g finely shredded Gruyère, plus more for sprinkling

¼ teaspoon freshly ground black pepper

small pinch of freshly grated nutmeg

1. Preheat the oven to 200°C/gas mark 6. Line two baking sheets with greaseproof paper, or if you're the sort to have silicone baking mats around the house, those are even better. Set the baking sheets aside.

2. In a medium saucepan, combine 120ml water with the milk, butter and salt and bring to the boil. Add the flour and stir it with a wooden spoon until a smooth dough forms. Turn the heat to low and continue stirring vigorously until the dough dries out and pulls away from the pan, about 2 minutes. If you have a stand mixer, plug that baby in.

3. Scrape the dough into the bowl of the stand mixer and let it cool for 1 minute. Fit the mixer with the paddle attachment, turn the machine to medium speed and add the eggs one at a time – and I do mean one at a time, chaps – beating them in thoroughly between each addition. Add the cheese, pepper and a pinch of nutmeg, then mix for a further minute. All this can also be done by hand, tedious as it may be.

4. Get out a pastry bag; if you don't have a pastry bag, jerry-rig one by cutting the corner off a 4-litre ziplock bag. Now fit the bag with a 13mm round tip – this one we can't get around, so you'll have to go and purchase a pastry tip if you don't already have one (remember how I said to read the recipe first?). Fill the pastry bag with dough and pipe tablespoon-size mounds onto the baking sheets a couple of inches apart.

5. Sprinkle the dough with cheese and bake for 22 minutes, or until puffed and golden brown. Serve hot, or cool them to room temperature, freeze them in a ziplock bag and reheat them in a preheated 180°C/gas mark 4 oven until piping hot.

HOMEMADE SAUSAGE ROLLS

A simple recipe like this one is all about buying some good-quality ingredients and then filling the house up with wicked aromas ASAP. I could give you a hundred different sausage recipes that you probably would never even read, and the truth is that most professional kitchens don't even make their own puff pastry anymore. So why fuck about wasting everyone's time? Let's make it easy, bake it fresh and make it yours.

SERVES 6

2 tablespoons extra virgin olive oil

1 onion, finely chopped

1 tablespoon chopped fresh sage

6 (115g) fresh pork sausages (never frozen!)

handful of dried breadcrumbs

tiny pinch of freshly grated nutmeg

4 sheets ready-made puff pastry

1 medium organic egg

a bit of milk

1. Preheat the oven to 180°C/gas mark 4 and cover a baking sheet with greaseproof paper.

2. Heat the oil in a medium saucepan over a medium heat and add the onion. Cook until soft and golden brown, about 5 minutes. Add the sage and cook for a further couple of minutes, then spread the mixture out onto a plate or baking sheet to cool off.

3. Using a sharp knife, slit the skins of the sausages and pop the meat out into a large bowl along with the cooled sage and onion mixture, the breadcrumbs, and nutmeg. Mix well with your (preferably clean) hands until evenly combined.

4. Hopefully your puff pastry came ready-sheeted; if not, on a floured work surface, roll the pastry out to form four 20 × 25cm rectangles about 3mm thick. Cut each lengthways into two even rectangles about 10cm wide. Now roll the sausage mixture into eight long tubes and place each in the centre of a piece of pastry dough.

5. Create an egg wash by whisking together the egg and milk. Brush the exposed surfaces of the pastry with the egg wash, then fold it up to wrap the sausage inside. Press down gently to seal.

6. Cut the long sausage rolls into the sizes you want (bigger is not always better) and space them out on the baking sheet. Brush the rolls with the rest of the egg wash and bake them in the oven for about 20 minutes, until golden brown and cooked through. Serve hot, ideally with Walnut Mustard (page 29) and, to make a meal of it, Butterhead Lettuce Salad (page 121).

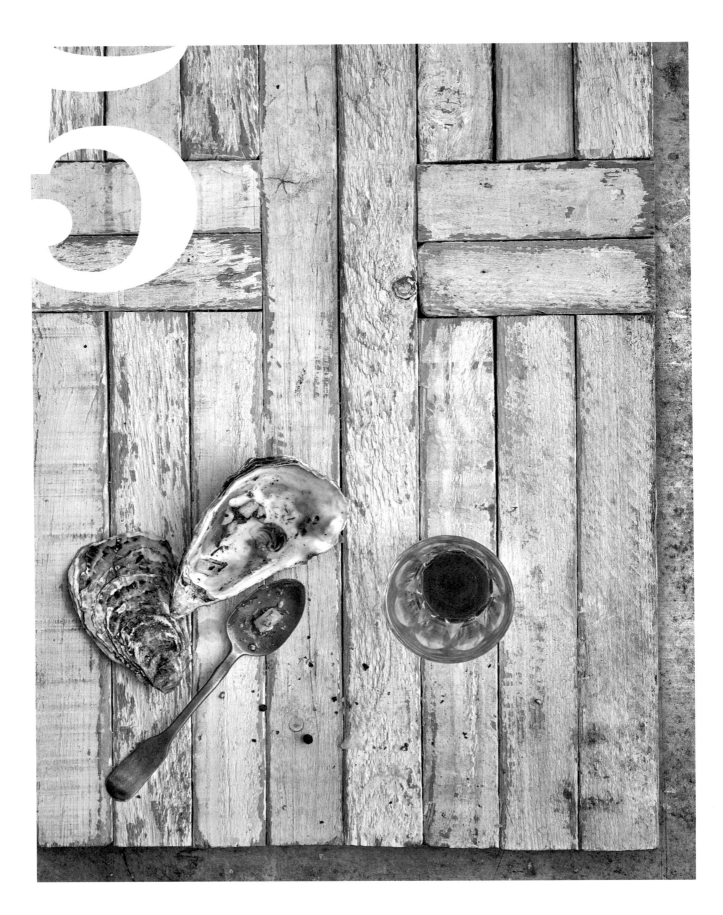

FISHES

WHEN I WAS A CHILD I HATED FISH, AND I ALWAYS KNEW WHEN WE WERE HAVING it for dinner because I could smell it all the way from the garden. To this day I have issues with salmon, because my granny would cook the life out of it and mash it, skin, bones and all, into a sandwich filling. I get the sense that a lot of people are still recovering from their own fish phobias instilled by horrible childhood eating experiences (sorry, mums) and need to be coaxed back into buying and cooking our finned friends.

What is it about fish that intimidates people so? I've seen grown men cower in front of the seafood counter, utterly confused by what to buy and how on earth they'll cook it once they get it home. This is a shame, because even with all the concerns today about sustainability and overfishing, seafood remains one of the best things you can feed yourself. It's delicious, good for you and carries a much smaller environmental impact than land meats such as beef and pork. We should all be eating more fish, full stop.

Most people avoid cooking fish at home because they're worried that they're going to mess it up: undercook it, overcook it or break it to mush in the pan. In this chapter, I provide a series of dead simple methods for preparing all types of seafood. Once you've mastered these techniques – from milk poaching, to baking to pan roasting – you'll be able to handle pretty much anything the seafood counter can throw at you.

WHOLE FISH IN FOIL

This recipe deserves a place on the greatest hits album without a doubt. It's very straightforward, hard to ruin with overcooking (everybody's worst fish cookery fear), and won't make your house smell like low tide. It also leaves you with a natural fish stock that can quickly be made into a butter sauce, making it mega-efficient for about fifteen minutes of prep time. It works for any whole fish small enough to fit inside a sheet of foil or greaseproof paper.

SERVES 2

1 × 1.1kg snapper or bass, scaled and gutted (look for fish with bright, wet eyes and pink gills)

coarse sea salt

a good drizzle of extra virgin olive oil

1 lemon, thinly sliced

1 large shallot, chopped

2 fresh bay leaves (dried can be substituted)

1 bundle assorted fresh herbs, such as thyme, rosemary, tarragon and parsley, plus some extra to bed the fish on while cooking

4 garlic cloves, crushed with the back of a knife

500ml good-quality dry white wine, plus extra for drinking

85g unsalted cold butter, diced

freshly ground black pepper

fresh lemon juice

1. Preheat the oven to 200°C/gas mark 6.

2. With a sharp knife, cut 3 diagonal incisions about 1cm deep into both sides of the fish. Season the fish generously with salt all over and drizzle with oil inside and out. Place a few lemon slices, the shallot, bay leaves, bundle of mixed herbs, and 2 of the garlic cloves inside the fish.

3. Lay out a large piece of foil or greaseproof paper on top of a baking sheet, and in the centre make a bed of the remaining herbs, lemon slices and garlic. Place the fish on top. Gather the foil or greaseproof paper above the fish, folding it together to make a packet but leaving a small opening. Add the wine, then seal the foil completely.

4. Roast until the fish is just cooked through, 30–35 minutes. Remove it from the oven, open one end of the foil, and carefully (with a capital C!) pour off the liquid into a small saucepan. Bring it to the boil over a high heat and reduce it by one third, 5–10 minutes. Turn the heat down to a slow simmer and whisk in the cold butter. Adjust the seasoning with salt, pepper and a drop or two of lemon juice.

5. To fillet the fish, insert your knife just below the fish's head and run it along the spine toward the tail, lifting off the top fillet. Now grab hold of the tail and carefully lift the spine and ribs off the bottom fillet. For an extra flourish, fillet the big boy tableside. By the way, this is how you butcher any round fish, from trout to bass to cod, pike, snapper and salmon.

6. Douse with your delicious pan sauce and serve.

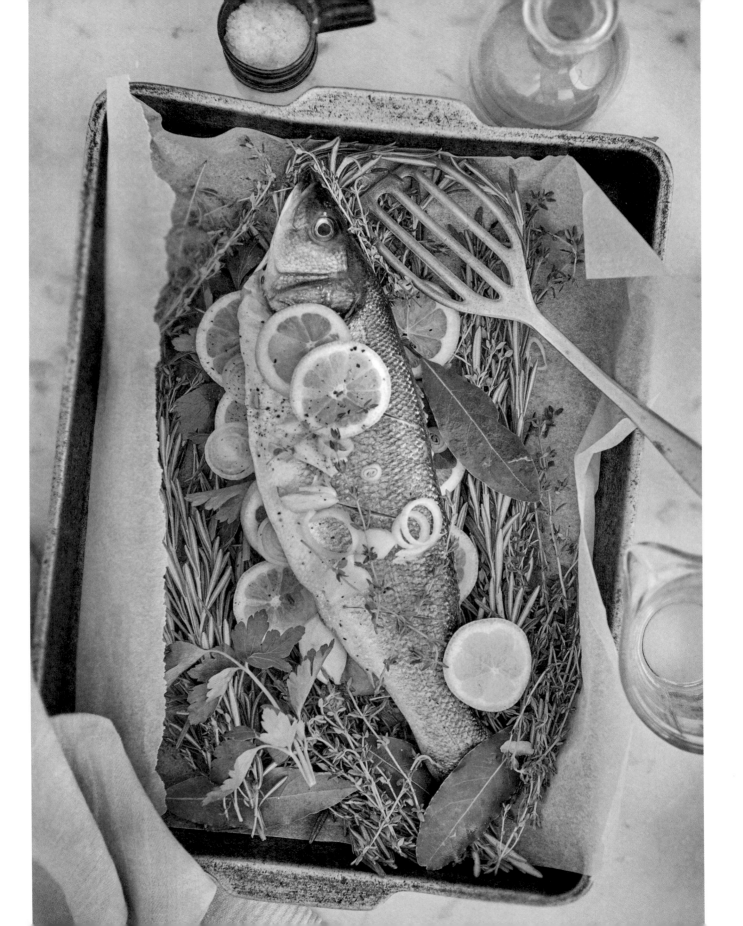

FISH AND CHIPS

As a British chef, I've spent the past decade trying to avoid being reduced and pigeonholed to a fish and chips fry cook. I've filled my menus with the likes of hand-cut pastas, house-made charcuterie, and delicate, Japanese-style crudos, relegating the fish fry to the specials board. Just when I thought I had escaped the stereotype, I stopped making fish and chips altogether and was graciously but thoroughly reamed by my restaurant guests. So, in the interest of keeping everyone happy, here's my recipe. It's a good one. Expect gratitude for making it once and abuse if you don't make it again. Don't say I didn't warn you.

SERVES 4

2 teaspoons dried active yeast

240ml warm water

¼ teaspoon paprika

¼ teaspoon ground turmeric

500ml beer, plus more for drinking

2 teaspoons malt vinegar

130g plain flour, plus more for dredging

100g cornflour

sea salt

1 medium egg white, whisked to medium peaks

rapeseed oil for frying

4 × 170g fillets fresh cod, haddock or halibut

Triple-Cooked Chips (page 141)

Tartare Sauce (recipe opposite)

1 lemon, quartered

1. Make the batter: Activate the yeast by mixing it with the warm water in a small bowl. Let it sit for a couple of minutes to start working, then add the paprika and turmeric. In a medium bowl, combine the beer and vinegar, then slowly whisk in the flour and cornflour. Once the yeast mixture is bubbly, add it to the batter. Season the batter with a generous pinch of salt, then fold in the whisked egg white.

2. Now we're going to make a deep-fryer. If you've got an electric one by chance, use it, because they're way safer; if not, take a heavy-based pan like a Dutch oven and fill it half full with oil. Position a thermometer in the oil and heat it nice and slow over a medium heat until the temperature reads 180°C. Drop a bit of batter carefully into the oil; it should sizzle immediately.

3. Standing over your fryer, dip a piece of cod in the batter twice, ensuring that the entire fish is well coated. If you have a fryer basket, use it; lay the fish gently into the oil and lift the fryer basket up, giving it a gentle shake to prevent the fish from settling on the bottom. If you don't have a fryer basket, lay the fish on a slotted spoon and lower it gently just below the surface of the oil, allowing the batter to crisp for 30 seconds or so before carefully removing the spoon. We're trying to keep the fish from dropping immediately to the bottom of the pan, where it will stick and fall apart if the batter hasn't crisped yet. Cook the fish for 4–5 minutes, until deep golden. Remove it to kitchen paper and repeat the process with the remaining fish.

4. While the fish is resting, fry your chips for their second time; remove them to kitchen paper and hit them with a generous sprinkle of salt. Divide the fish and chips among 4 plates and serve them with a bowl of tartare sauce and lemon quarters.

TARTARE SAUCE

MAKES 400ML

180ml mayonnaise

¼ small yellow onion, finely diced

2 tablespoons superfine capers, rinsed (finely chopped normal capers can be substituted)

6 caper berries, stemmed and diced (these are larger than capers and have stems)

50g cornichons, finely diced

2 tablespoons chopped fresh chives

2 tablespoons chopped fresh flat-leaf parsley

Mix everything together in a small bowl.

THE POWER OF THE BRINE

Brining fish may sound just a bit redundant – this is an animal that spent its whole life swimming around in brine, after all – but it's my secret weapon for fish cookery. Soaking fish in a saltwater solution firms up its flesh and seasons it throughout, extracting excess water and leaving just a pure flavour of fish behind. Brining allows the fillets or steaks to get really crisp when baked or sautéed, because they sear against the hot pan instead of steaming in their own juices.

To make a brine suitable for any and all fish, mix together a solution that's one fifth salt and four fifths water, plus a big pinch of sugar. Add aromatics that work well with fish, such as lemon zest, parsley and thyme. Heat the liquid just to dissolve the salt and sugar, then chill it in the fridge until cold. Brine your fish for 35 minutes, rinse it, then let it dry out in the fridge between kitchen paper for at least 25 minutes. The surface of the fish should be dry to the touch. Now it's ready to cook; no additional seasoning necessary.

BAKED HALIBUT

Everyone just loves halibut, probably because, like tuna, it tastes a bit like meat; it's one of the least 'fishy' fish in the ocean. During halibut season, I cook with it non-stop. This recipe also works for cod, flounder, sole – any skinless white fish. Just don't ever, ever buy tilapia. It tastes like garbage and is, for the most part, raised in squalor in Chinese fish farms.

One of the best ways to cook lean, flaky white fish is in a slow oven, which cooks it through gently without drying out – as well as avoiding the sad fate of falling to shreds in a frying pan. Use a toothpick or skewer to tell when thicker fillets of fish are cooked through: when you think the fish is done, stab it with the toothpick. If it meets with resistance, the fish is still raw in the middle. If it moves through the flesh easily, you're in good shape.

SERVES 4

2 tablespoons chopped fresh chives

1 teaspoon lemon zest

1 tablespoon finely diced fresh ginger

4 tablespoons olive oil

4 × 170g halibut fillets, each about 4cm thick

1 teaspoon coarse sea salt

¾ teaspoon freshly ground black pepper

lemon wedges for garnish (optional)

1. Preheat the oven to 160°C/gas mark 3.

2. Make the topping: mix the chives, lemon zest, ginger and 2 tablespoons of the oil in a small bowl. Cover and chill. This can be prepared 4 hours ahead, but keep it cold.

3. Place the fillets on a baking sheet and coat them all over with the remaining 2 tablespoons oil. Sprinkle the tops of the fillets with the salt, pepper and chive-lemon topping, giving it a good press so that it sticks. Bake the fish just until cooked through, 9–10 minutes. Serve immediately with the lime wedges.

MILK-POACHED SMOKED SALMON

This dish has a vaguely trendy feel to it, owing to the Nordic fondness for smoked fish and for whey poaching: a technique for slowly cooking meats and fishes in the tangy liquid by-product of cheese making. The difference is that I use milk instead of whey, and I've been poaching smoked salmon in it since Rene Redzepi was still reading comic books under his bed.

Notice that we're using hot-smoked, or 'kippered' salmon in this recipe. So, not the cold-smoked, translucent, thinly sliced stuff that you get in vacuum packs at the grocery shop and put on top of bagels. Hot-smoked salmon is meaty, opaque, flaky and sold in fillets. It's less common than the cold-smoked variety, so you're going to have to go somewhere with a decent smoked fish selection to find it.

SERVES 4

1 litre whole milk

Some parsley stalks
(minus the leaves)

1 bay leaf

4 × 170g skin-on hot-smoked salmon portions

170g Herb Butter (page 35)

1 bag prewashed
spinach leaves

coarse sea salt and freshly
ground black pepper

1. Find a pan about 10cm deep and big enough in diameter to comfortably hold the salmon portions. Add the milk and 120ml water, a few parsley stalks and the bay leaf. Bring it to the boil over a high heat; the water should stop the milk from scorching. Turn the heat down to a gentle simmer and add the salmon.

2. Poach the salmon for 5 minutes, or until it's cooked to a medium temperature throughout. The salmon should retain some pinkness, and the skin should peel off with a gentle pull. Remove it to a kitchen paper-lined plate and allow the excess milk to drain off. Place a small pat of herb butter on top of each fillet and allow it to melt.

3. In a large sauté pan over a medium-low heat, melt the remaining herb butter. Once it begins to foam, add the spinach and sauté it until wilted. Season with salt and pepper.

4. Divide the spinach among four plates and top with the salmon fillets.

GRILLED OYSTERS WITH CURRIED APPLE BUTTER

Raw oysters tend to be a 'love it or hate it' food, and personally, I've never been a huge fan. I struggle to understand why people don't cook them more often. Grilled with a knob of spiced butter on top, their flesh firms up and caramelises as it roasts. That signature, briny flavour is balanced out by the richness of the butter. What's not to like?

SERVES 4–6

115g unsalted
butter, softened

½ teaspoon Madras
curry powder

¼ teaspoon smoked
Spanish paprika

¼ teaspoon cayenne pepper

1 tablespoon chopped
fresh coriander

2 tablespoons peeled,
finely diced apple,
preferably Granny Smith

a squeeze of lemon juice

a dash of coarse sea salt
and grind of black pepper

1 dozen large oysters, such
as Colchester or Cornish

sea salt

1. In a medium bowl, combine the butter, curry powder, paprika, cayenne, coriander, apple, lemon juice, salt and pepper and mix them up with a spatula or wooden spoon until evenly combined.

2. Heat your grill for medium-high-heat cooking. Crack open the oysters and discard the top halves of each shell. Detach the oysters from their bottom shells and turn the meat upside down so that the plump side faces up. Set them on a baking sheet atop little mounds of sea salt, which will keep them from tipping over.

3. Spoon a level teaspoon of the butter mixture on top of each oyster. Place them under the grill and cook them for 3–4 minutes, until the butter is melted and begins to caramelise.

4. Crack open a beer and scarf them down hot.

OYSTERS 101

If you're gearing up to shuck oysters at home, there's likely just one question at the top of your mind: how will I know if I get a bad one?

Trust me, you'll know. The oyster will feel light for its size. The shell might be brittle and flaky. There will be a lack of liquor inside, or what's there will look milky rather than clear. The oyster itself will be dry and wrinkled. The smell will be off; fishy, not fresh and sweet. And if by some chance you still decide to try the bloody thing, it will taste metallic and rancid. But really, don't try it.

The best way to avoid bad oysters has to do with how you buy them. Getting them shipped direct from the oyster farm is ideal, as you know they'll be just two to three days out of the water. If you're picking them up at a seafood counter, you want to know their harvest date. Avoid anything that's been out of the water for a week or more.

Once you get your oysters home, store them cup-side down in as cold a place as possible. If your fridge isn't 1°C or below, chuck some ice on top of them to help chill them down. Don't ever put oysters in the freezer, though. They need to be kept alive until you eat them.

The fastest way to open a small oyster is to stick the tip of a paring knife right into the hinge and twist it to open the shell. A dull-tipped oyster knife is definitely the safer alternative, and therefore I'll make that my official recommendation. No matter what you use and what sort of oyster you're opening, be sure to wedge the knife as deeply into the oyster's hinge as possible before you start prying it open. Smaller oysters tend to be easier to open, but this isn't always the case.

There are loads of oyster varieties out there, and whether you want Colchester, Cornish, Loch Ryan, West Mersea or any other kind all comes down to personal preference. There's no 'best' variety. Oysters differ in flavour and texture based on the species as well as where they grow.

PAN-ROASTED SALMON

The number one mistake that people make when cooking fish on the hob is – gather round close, now – not letting the pan get hot enough before adding the fish. If that metal isn't really, properly blazing hot, the fish will stick to it like molasses and proceed to fall apart when you try to flip it (sound familiar?). So go on, throw open a window, turn the venting on high, take the battery out of your smoke detector if you dare, and wait for the oil to shimmer and smoke before you move a muscle.

Equipment is also key. Use a pan with a non-stick surface: cast iron, black steel or Teflon all work. An easy rule of thumb is to pick a pan with a dark cooking surface. Aluminium or stainless steel won't do. Finally, be sure to leave the fish alone until it releases from the pan on its own, rather than trying to scrape it up and flip it just because the timer's gone off.

Follow these three guidelines and you have a fighting chance of not fucking up.

SERVES 4

2 tablespoons grapeseed or vegetable oil

4 × 170g skin-on centre cut salmon fillets

coarse sea salt

freshly ground black pepper

½ lemon

1. Preheat the oven to 180°C/gas mark 4.

2. Heat the oil in a large, ovenproof cast iron, black steel or Teflon frying pan over a medium-high heat. Dry off the salmon fillets between sheets of kitchen paper and season them with salt (never add pepper at this stage: pepper burns).

3. Once the pan is piping hot and the oil has begun to smoke, add the salmon skin-side down. Press gently on the fillets with a spatula to ensure that the skin is in full contact with the pan and cook without touching it until the skin is golden and crisp, about 5 minutes.

4. Transfer the pan to the oven and roast the salmon until opaque, 4–5 minutes. The exact timing will depend on the thickness of the fillets; it should measure 52°C in the centre. Remove it from the oven, quickly turn over the salmon and spoon the cooking oil over the top a couple of times. Divide the fillets among four plates. Season with a little salt, a grind of pepper and a squeeze of lemon and serve.

SMOKED SALMON AND POTATO TERRINE WITH SAUCE GRIBICHE

This terrine is a pain in the bollocks to make. It takes time, skill and a good amount of patience. But it's delicious and looks spectacular as a starter, brunch dish or part of a truly impressive charcuterie board. What can I say; cooking needn't always be about what's quick and sensible. So, man up! Get your tape measure out and start laying down salmon and potatoes.

MAKES ONE 20 × 10CM TERRINE

4 large Maris Piper
potatoes or other
large waxy potatoes

sea salt

½ full side sliced smoked
Scottish salmon (I really
like Scottish salmon)

Anchovy Butter
(recipe opposite)

Sauce Gribiche
(recipe opposite)

1. Peel the potatoes and slice them paper-thin, about 1.5mm thick. If you have a little meat slicer or a mandoline (the slicer, not the mini guitar), this is a good time to dust it off and use it. Watch your fingers.

2. Fill a large saucepan two thirds full with salted water and bring it to the boil. Add the sliced potatoes and simmer until soft but not falling apart, 15–20 minutes. Remove the pan from the heat and allow the potatoes to cool in the water to room temperature, about 30 minutes (this part is important; if you drain them while hot, they'll fall to pieces). Remove the potatoes from the water with a slotted spoon and dry them using kitchen paper.

3. Line a terrine mould or loaf tin about 40 × 10cm in size with clingfilm, leaving enough of an overhang on all sides to completely cover the top of the terrine when folded. Now line the bottom and inside walls of the terrine with the largest pieces of smoked salmon, covering all five sides without allowing the pieces to overlap. Brush the bottom with anchovy butter.

4. Your potatoes should now be dry, and here's where the tape measure comes in: you need to cover the bottom of the terrine perfectly with potato slices that have been measured and trimmed appropriately, like building a stone wall – no gaps or overlaps. Then brush the potatoes with anchovy butter. Cover the potatoes with a single layer of smoked salmon and brush it with anchovy butter. Repeat with the remaining potatoes and smoked salmon until the terrine is full to the brim, finishing with a layer of salmon on top. My best time for this is 18 minutes, so add an hour on to that and you should be good.

5. Fold any overhanging salmon over the top of the terrine, followed by the clingfilm. Wrap the whole terrine in a few more layers of clingfilm until it's very tightly sealed, then press down on it as hard as you can to force any air out (you can also put it on the floor and stand on it – just don't fall over). Refrigerate the terrine for at least 2 hours and up to a week.

6. Remove the terrine from its mould and rewrap it tightly in fresh clingfilm to help it hold its shape when sliced (It's a bit fragile, so a really sharp knife will come in handy). Cut it into 1cm slices, and make sure you have plenty of mates around to show off to. Serve with a bowl of Sauce Gribiche on the side.

ANCHOVY BUTTER
MAKES ABOUT 250ML

225g unsalted butter
3–4 anchovy fillets
1 tablespoon chopped fresh parsley

1. Place the butter in a microwave-safe bowl. Heat it for 10 seconds at a time in the microwave until it liquefies but the butterfat has not separated from the butter solids.

2. Finely chop the anchovies to a fine paste, then add them along with the parsley into the liquefied butter and whisk until evenly combined.

SAUCE GRIBICHE
MAKES 240ML

2 tablespoons finely chopped cornichons or small pickles
2 tablespoons finely chopped capers
½ teaspoon chopped fresh parsley
½ teaspoon chopped fresh tarragon
½ teaspoon chopped fresh chives
½ teaspoon chopped fresh chervil
115g mayonnaise
1 egg, hard-boiled and chopped

In a medium bowl, mix all the ingredients until well combined. This sauce can be made a day in advance and stored in the fridge.

SALMON ON A CEDAR PLANK

I've written three different salmon recipes into this book, and it's not because salmon is my favourite fish. But it's incredibly popular and widely available, so I figure you ought to have a few good ways to cook it in your back pocket. This easy cedar plank method keeps the fish from drying out and flavours it gently with the warm scent of cedar. If you don't fancy grilling, it can just as easily be done in a 150°C/gas mark 2 oven.

SERVES 4

coarse sea salt

4 × 170–225g salmon fillets

freshly ground
black pepper

6 tablespoons
Dijon mustard

6 tablespoons maple
sugar (brown sugar
may be substituted)

1 lemon, cut in half

1. Soak a cedar plank about 15 × 35cm in size in lightly salted water for 2 hours. Drain.

2. Remove the skin from each salmon fillet and season both sides well with salt and pepper. Place the fillets on the cedar plank and brush the tops and sides liberally with mustard. Sprinkle them evenly with the maple sugar.

3. Prepare your grill for indirect heat cooking; for a gas grill, this means lighting only half of it, and for a charcoal grill it means banking the coals to one side. While the grill is heating, place the salmon and plank on the side of the grill away from the flame and drop the cover of the grill. The temperature should be around 150°C. Cook the fish for 15–20 minutes; the internal temperature of the salmon should read 52°C for medium rare, which is how I like it. If you want it medium-well, leave it for another 5–10 minutes.

4. Remove the fish from the grill and squeeze lemon juice over the fillets. Serve them right off the plank, with potatoes and salad.

QUINOA AND SHELLFISH PAELLA

Each summer growing up the Collinses had our two weeks somewhere warm in mainland Europe to get sunburnt and sleep late. One year, on a trip to the island of Majorca, my mum was adamant that we experience the local culture. I immediately took to Spanish food – it's hard not to like crispy-fried *patatas bravas*, oozing *croquetas*, and Serrano ham, after all – but wasn't so sure about the paella. Rice was still a novelty in 1980s Britain, and it wasn't for me. Years later, when I moved to the States and discovered quinoa, I knew that it would make a perfect substitute. It might fly in the face of tradition, but I find quinoa easier to eat than rice and really dig how it absorbs all the dish's delicious flavours while adding a pleasing crunch.

SERVES 4

1 tablespoon extra virgin olive oil

1 large onion, diced

1 carrot, diced

1 stick celery, diced

1 leek, diced

4 piquillo peppers, diced

2 medium tomatoes, diced

2 garlic cloves, finely chopped

115g Spanish chorizo, diced

170g quinoa, rinsed

1 teaspoon curry powder

¼ teaspoon Spanish paprika

240ml white wine

240ml bottle clam juice or fish stock

115g raw large prawns, peeled and deveined

170g clams

170g mussels

115g cooked lobster meat, chopped

115g fresh scallops

2 tablespoons chopped fresh flat–leaf parsley

1 teaspoon chopped fresh dill

2 tablespoons chopped fresh coriander

salt and freshly ground black pepper

1 tablespoon fresh lemon juice

1. In a Dutch oven over medium-high, heat the oil until it shimmers. Chuck in the diced vegetables and cook for 5 minutes, or until they're soft and beginning to colour. Add the garlic, chorizo, quinoa and spices and cook for a further 5 minutes.

2. Stir in the wine and let it reduce by half. Add the clam juice or fish stock, cover the pan with a lid, reduce the heat, and let it slowly simmer for about 15 minutes.

3. Now add the prawns and stir them around for 30 seconds, or until they begin to turn pink. Add the clams and mussels, cover the pan and cook for about 4 minutes, until the shells open.

4. Stir the lobster and scallops into the quinoa; you're basically just warming them through and lightly cooking the scallops. Stir in the chopped fresh herbs and season the dish with salt, pepper and the lemon juice. Drizzle a little bit of oil over the top, place the pan in the middle of the table, and serve.

SQUID INK CAPPELLINI WITH LOBSTER BOLOGNESE

This dish has been on my menus for years, and during that time has developed a solid fan following. In the restaurant, we make a rich stock from lobster shells and use that as the basis for the Bolognese sauce; for the home cook, you can save yourself a lot of hard work by buying a jar of concentrated 'lobster base', which reconstitutes in hot water into stock (hey, I won't tell if you won't . . .). If you're not up to making the squid ink pasta, any regular store-bought cappellini will do. Truth be told, though, the squid ink pasta really makes the dish for me, so why not borrow a pasta machine and give it a go? Either way, it's rock star pasta, and a very solid move for date night with the missus.

SERVES 4–6

4 tablespoons vegetable oil

150g sliced or diced white mushrooms

1 small carrot, finely chopped

½ onion, finely chopped

3 sticks celery, finely chopped

1 leek, white part only, finely chopped

4 garlic cloves, finely chopped

coarse sea salt

1½ tablespoons lobster base or paste (optional)

1 tablespoon tomato purée

500ml white wine

800g tinned chopped tomatoes, preferably San Marzano tomatoes from Italy

170g unsalted butter

Squid Ink Cappellini (recipe follows) or shop-bought cappellini

280–340g cooked lobster tail meat, diced

a squeeze of lemon juice

1. Heat 1 tablespoon of the oil in a medium sauté pan set over a medium-high heat. Once the oil is shimmering, add the mushrooms and cook, stirring occasionally, until soft and golden brown, 5–7 minutes. Set them aside.

2. Heat the remaining 3 tablespoons oil in a 5- or 6-litre pan over a medium heat. Add the carrot, onion, celery, leek and garlic to the pan and season with a large pinch of salt. Sweat the vegetables slowly, letting them release their juices without colouring, 2–3 minutes.

3. Stir in the lobster base, if using, and tomato purée and cook for 3 minutes. Add the wine and scrape the browned bits off the surface of the pan while it bubbles (this is called *deglazing*). Reduce the wine until nearly dry, 5–10 minutes, then add the tomatoes.

4. Simmer the sauce slowly over a medium-low heat for 30–45 minutes, stirring it frequently to ensure that it doesn't stick to the bottom of the pan and burn. Remove it from the heat and stir through the butter.

5. Meanwhile, bring 4 litres of seawater-salty water to the boil. Drop the fresh pasta in and cook it for 2 minutes. Lift the pasta from the water with tongs, transfer it to the tomato sauce, and cook it for a further 30–45 seconds. Add the cooked mushrooms and lobster meat and cook for 1 minute, just to heat the lobster through. Taste and add salt as needed. Using tongs, lift the pasta from the pan into bowls. Squeeze a bit of lemon juice over the top and serve.

SQUID INK CAPPELLINI

MAKES 450G

210g '00' pasta flour

pinch of sea salt

2 medium whole eggs

3 medium egg yolks

½ teaspoon olive oil

½ tablespoon squid ink

semolina flour (optional)

1. Combine the flour and salt in a food processor. Crack the eggs and yolks into a small cup and whisk in the oil and squid ink. With the food processor running, add the egg mixture to the flour in a quick stream. Give the machine a good shake to bring everything together to form a loose, crumbly dough. Dump it all out onto a work surface and, using your hands, press the dough into a shaggy single mass.

2. Start to knead the dough with your right hand by folding the back edge toward you, and then pushing it down and away with the heel of your hand. Turn the dough a quarter turn and repeat for 5–10 minutes. You'll know the dough has been kneaded properly when it has formed into a smooth, elastic mass and bounces back when you press it with your finger.

3. Wrap the dough in clingfilm and place it in the fridge to rest for at least 30 minutes but ideally overnight.

4. Dust a baking sheet with flour, preferably semolina flour, or if not, '00' pasta flour. Roll the dough out using a pasta machine fitted with a cappellini attachment according to the manufacturer's instructions. Lay the strands of pasta flat on the sheet, dust them with flour, and let them sit at room temperature until you're ready to use them.

   Note: If you don't have food processor, you can make pasta dough using what is known as the 'well' method. Mix the flour and salt together on a work surface and create a well in the centre of the flour. Add the egg mixture and, working from the inner edges of the well outward, use a fork to slowly incorporate the flour into the liquid until everything is combined into a shaggy dough. Knead the dough as instructed above to produce your smooth elastic ball, wrap and place in the fridge to rest.

OCTOPUS SALAD

Congratulations! If you're reading this, it means you saw the word *octopus* and didn't immediately turn the page. Thanks for bearing with me.

In the wrong hands, octopus can be tough, rubbery and bland, but trust me that this Mediterranean-style salad is packed with flavour and not very difficult to pull off. In fact, the hardest part of this recipe will be finding somewhere to buy the octopus. After all, it's not the kind of thing you can just whistle up at your neighbourhood superstore. If you live in a city with a Chinatown, that's a good place to start. Otherwise, ask your nearest fishmonger to order one for you.

There are two ways to tenderise fresh octopus before cooking. You can either freeze and thaw it, or you can beat the shit out of it. Actually, make that three ways: the easiest option is to ask the guy who sold it to you to tenderise it for you. Otherwise, spend half an hour going Rocky on that octo, or perhaps flinging it against your garage door, in order to get the flesh nice and supple. You can also put it in the freezer and then let it defrost for a day in the fridge before use. Your call. It depends on how much repressed rage you've got on your hands.

SERVES 6

1 (900g) octopus

900g red-skinned potatoes, such as Desiree (about 6 medium potatoes)

coarse sea salt

1 whole garlic clove, peeled

1 bay leaf

½ tablespoon black peppercorns

120ml olive oil

5 tablespoons white wine vinegar

2 garlic cloves, crushed

freshly ground black pepper

leaves from 1 bunch flat-leaf parsley, chopped

1. Behead the octopus. Slit the head in half and turn it inside out to empty its contents and remove any loosely attached bits (such as the eyes). Remove the beak from the centre, where all of the tentacles meet. Rinse the octopus head and tentacles under cold running water.

2. Place the potatoes (whole and unpeeled) in a pressure cooker and add enough water to cover them halfway. Add a pinch of salt. Close and lock the lid and place it over a high heat. When the pan reaches pressure, reduce the heat to low and set a timer for 15 minutes. When the time is up, release all of the vapour from the pressure cooker and remove the potatoes with tongs, reserving the cooking water. Peel the potatoes while they are as hot as you can handle (the skin should slip off easily).

3. Add enough water to the pressure cooker to almost totally cover the octopus (eyeball it), plus the whole garlic clove, bay leaf and peppercorns and bring the water to the boil. Add the cleaned octopus head and tentacles. Close and lock the lid of the pressure cooker and turn the heat to high. Once it gets to pressure, reduce the heat to low and set a timer for 15 minutes. When the time is up, release all of the vapour and check the octopus for tenderness; a fork should sink easily into the thickest part of the flesh. If not, close the lid and bring it to pressure for another minute or two and check it again.

4. When the octopus is ready, remove it from the pressure cooker and drain off the liquid. Remove any remaining skin from the octopus by lightly dragging a knife blade on the back end and sides of the tentacles; only remove the skin from the suction-cup side if you want to remove the suction cups, which are a nice decorative flourish if you ask me. Chop up the head and tentacles into small, bite-size chunks.

5. Prepare a vinaigrette by combining the oil, vinegar, crushed garlic cloves and salt and pepper to taste in a small jar. Close the lid and shake it to blend.

6. Chop the potatoes into bite-size chunks and combine them in a bowl with the octopus, chopped parsley, and vinaigrette. Mix well and serve at room temperature.

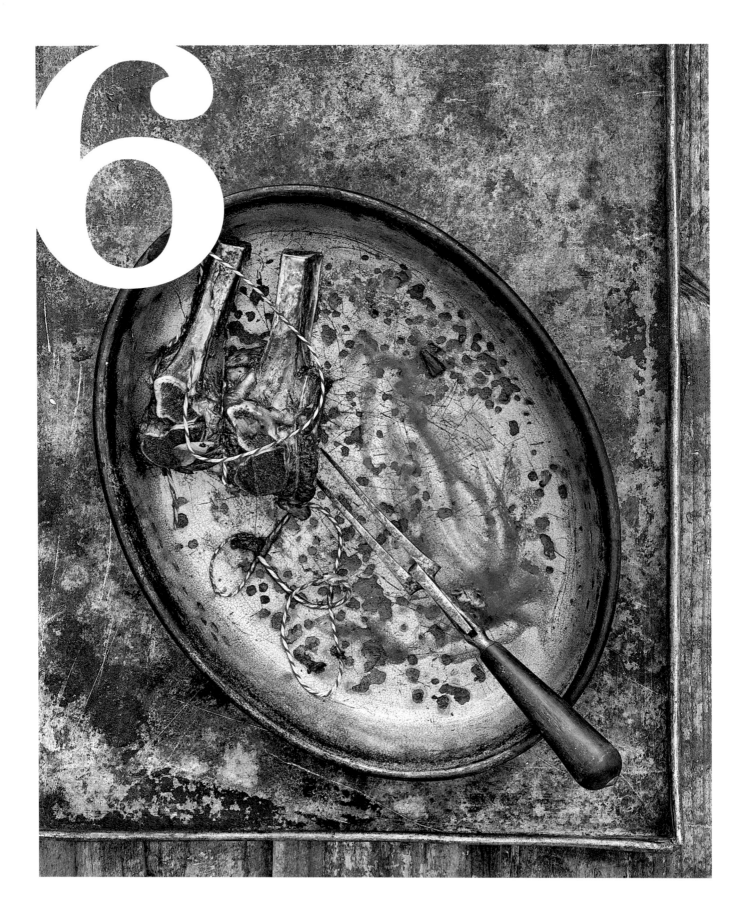

6

MEATS

EVERYTHING BUT THE QUACK

DUCK IS ONE OF MY FAVOURITE MEATS. Lighter than beef and pork and more flavourful than chicken, these little birds are fantastically tasty, forgiving to cook, and easier than ever to get your hands on. Still, though, I've seen little in the way of good duck recipes geared towards the home cook. So this chapter offers a few of my favourite uses for every part of the duck – including the eggs, which are big, rich and gorgeous, like chicken eggs on steroids.

DUCK PROSCIUTTO

We've touched on some charcuterie recipes already – all cooked or pressed stuff – but this is your big chance to cure your own meat. Duck breast is the easiest whole muscle to cure and dry, as it's small enough to do the whole process in a standard fridge. The texture and flavour are wonderfully distinct, and you can use duck prosciutto in loads of different ways, from charcuterie platters to sandwiches and salads. The process takes some patience, but it's cool as fuck knowing you can pull something like this off in your own kitchen.

You might have your doubts about whether you can really hang onto raw meat for upward of a month without it rotting. Well, the duck breasts won't rot, thanks to the salt-curing process. As you watch the breasts dry, keep in mind that white mould is good mould! If you see green mould, wash the afflicted breast in saltwater solution and re-hang it. But you won't get green mould unless it's living somewhere in your fridge already, which is another problem entirely.

MAKES 4 DUCK PROSCIUTTOS

4 × 280–340g Pekin or Muscovy duck breasts

2 ½ teaspoons black peppercorns

2½ teaspoons coriander seeds

1 teaspoon fennel seeds

pinch of juniper berries

2 pinches of Szechuan peppercorns (optional)

300g coarse sea salt

1 teaspoon pink curing salt (also called Prague powder No. 2)

170g granulated sugar

1. Weigh each duck breast and record the weights someplace where you won't lose it.

2. In a small saucepan set over a medium heat, toast the black peppercorns, coriander seeds, fennel seeds, juniper berries and Szechuan peppercorns, if using, until fragrant, 1–2 minutes.

3. Coarsely crack the toasted spices using a pestle and mortar or a coffee grinder. Chuck them into a small bowl and mix them thoroughly with the salts and sugar. Pack the duck breasts on all sides with this dry cure, then bury them in the remaining cure inside a sealed plastic container or ziplock bag.

4. Cure the breasts for 24 hours, then remove them from the curing mixture and brush off as much as possible with a tea towel. Let the breasts dry uncovered in the refrigerator for 8 hours.

5. Take a length of butcher's twine and tie one end around each breast, or poke a hole in one end of each breast, thread the twine through, and tie a loop. Hang the breasts from a rack in the fridge until each breast has lost at least 20–25 per cent of its weight, 4–6 weeks. Thinly slice and serve. It will keep stored in the fridge for up to 6 months.

DUCK AND WALNUT TERRINE

I know what you're thinking: 'Yeah, right! Good one, knobhead, as if I'm going to bother making this.' But this terrine is proper worth it. And it gets better with a bit of age, as all the flavours meld. It's good to eat as soon as it's chilled, two weeks on it's great and after three it's fantastic. At the one-month mark, though, you should probably get rid of it.

MAKES ONE 20 × 10CM TERRINE

115g duck leg meat, diced

55g pork shoulder
meat, diced

40g pork back fat

30g chicken livers

½ teaspoon coarse sea salt

¼ teaspoon freshly
ground black pepper

¼ teaspoon
granulated sugar

½ garlic clove,
finely chopped

½ shallot, diced

½ teaspoon fresh
thyme leaves

2 tablespoons brandy

2 tablespoons port

2 slices white bread

120ml double cream

35g walnut pieces

¼ teaspoon pink curing
salt (also called Prague
powder No. 2)

20g foie gras, diced

40g duck breast, diced

1. In a large bowl, combine the duck leg meat, pork shoulder, back fat, chicken livers, coarse sea salt, black pepper, sugar, garlic, shallot, thyme, brandy and port. Toss well and cover. Refrigerate for 24 hours. Remove the meat mixture from the fridge, drain it through a fine-mesh sieve, and discard the liquid.

2. Preheat the oven to 160°C/gas mark 3.

3. Using a stand mixer with a meat grinder attachment fitted with a coarse plate, grind the meat once through into a large bowl. In a blender, combine the white bread and cream and blend until smooth. Add the bread mixture to the ground meat, followed by the walnuts, curing salt, foie gras and duck breast. Mix it up well with your hands.

4. Line the bottom and sides of a large earthenware terrine or 20 × 10cm loaf tin with clingfilm, leaving enough of an overhang on all sides of the tin so that the clingfilm will completely cover the top of the pâté mixture when folded over. Transfer the meat mixture to the terrine mould, pressing it down with your fingers to make sure it's tightly packed. Fold the overlapping clingfilm over the mixture to encase it. Use a piece of cardboard or a bit of wood to press down so the meat is packed nice and even and you've got out all the excess air.

5. Set the terrine mould in a roasting tin and add boiling water to reach three quarters of the way up the sides. Bake for 1 hour 30 minutes, or until the internal temperature reaches 74°C. Remove the terrine from the oven, wrap it in foil, then place a 1–1.35kg weight on top of it; this is called pressing, and it's very important for packing the pâté nice and tight, removing any air that would cause the pâté to discolour and go bad during the maturing process.

6. Refrigerate the terrine for at least 8 hours. Cut it into 1cm slices and serve.

ROASTED DUCK BREAST WITH FIGS AND FARRO

Duck is always a big seller on restaurant menus, but for some reason, it doesn't occur to people to cook it for themselves at home. This is a shame, because how much beef, turkey, chicken and pork can you choke down before getting sick to death of it? Sure, duck is more expensive than chicken, but it's also cheaper than a good-quality steak. And the truth is that duck breast is easier to cook than almost anything, thanks to the ample layer of fat that keeps the meat naturally moist and tender while it roasts.

This is a dish with a restaurant-quality feel, but an ease and simplicity to the execution that makes it perfect for banging out at home. It's a great choice when company's coming. Farro, for those unfamiliar, is a type of whole grain wheat that can be prepared like a risotto. Fresh figs are available throughout the year; if you can't get them, substitute an equal volume of apricots, peaches, apples or pears.

SERVES 4

4 × 280–340g duck breasts, ideally Pekin or Muscovy

4 tablespoons dry sherry

4 tablespoons sherry vinegar

120ml chicken stock

2 teaspoons honey

1 teaspoon chopped fresh thyme

coarse sea salt and freshly ground black pepper

8 fresh figs, stemmed and cut in half

1 tablespoon unsalted butter

Farrotto (recipe follows)

1. Preheat the oven to 220°C/gas mark 7.

2. If your duck breasts still have sinew on them and the fat side hasn't been scored, your butcher is a wanker and you're going to have to do it yourself. With the skin side of the breast facing up, use a very sharp knife to cut through the skin and fat almost to the flesh, forming a grid pattern with the lines 3mm apart. Flip the breast over; if you see any silvery white skin, trim it off as carefully as you can, trying not to remove any meat.

3. Heat a large cast-iron pan over a medium-high heat for 1 minute, letting it get good and hot. Place the duck breasts in the pan skin-side down and let the fat begin to render – aka liquefy. After about 6 minutes, when the skin is golden brown, begin basting the tops of the breasts, spooning the rendered fat over. Continue basting and cooking until much of the fat is rendered and the skin is crisp and deep golden brown, a further 2–4 minutes.

4. Put the pan in the oven and roast the breasts until cooked through, 3–4 minutes. If you want to prod one with a thermometer, it should read 57°C in the centre for medium-rare, which is how I recommend serving duck. Transfer the duck breasts to a plate and cover them with foil to rest and keep warm.

5. Pour off the remaining fat and set the pan back on a medium-high heat. Add the sherry and sherry vinegar; scrape the pan with a wooden spoon to release the browned bits, then boil the liquid until reduced to 2 tablespoons, about 3 minutes. Add the stock, honey and thyme and season with salt and pepper. Boil until the liquid is reduced by about half, about 3 more minutes. Reduce the heat to low and add the figs. Add the butter to the sauce in bits, consistently stirring or swirling the pan.

6. Slice the duck opposite the grain of the muscle fibres into 2cm slices and arrange them on a bed of farrotto. Drizzle with the fig pan sauce and serve.

(continued)

FARROTTO

Wild rocket has smaller, spindlier, and more peppery leaves than farmed rocket. It can typically be found at farmers' markets and some supermarkets.

SERVES 4

105g farro

1.5 litres chicken stock

3 tablespoons olive oil

30g unsalted butter

1 large or 2 small shallots, chopped

coarse sea salt and freshly
ground black pepper

80ml white wine

45g diced fresh figs

30g pine nuts, toasted

3 handfuls of wild rocket (farmed
rocket can be substituted)

40g grated Parmesan

¼ lemon

1. In a medium bowl, soak the farro in 1 litre water for 30 minutes. Drain. Meanwhile, heat the stock in a small saucepan and keep it warm over a low heat.

2. In a large saucepan, heat the oil and butter over a medium heat until the butter begins to foam. Add the shallots and season with a pinch of salt and a grind of pepper. Cook until softened, about 2 minutes.

3. Add the drained farro and stir constantly until toasted, 3–4 minutes. Chuck in the wine and stir constantly until evaporated, about 2 minutes.

4. Begin adding the hot stock a ladleful at a time, stirring the farro constantly until the stock is completely absorbed. Keep adding stock, waiting until one addition is fully absorbed before adding more, until the farro is creamy and cooked through, about 30 minutes. Turn off the heat and stir in the figs, pine nuts, rocket and Parmesan. Season with salt, pepper and a squeeze of lemon juice.

DUCK AU VIN

Duck legs are truly delicious; they're basically poultry that thinks it's red meat. The way that people most commonly cook them is confit style, which means simmering them in duck fat. I've found that braising duck legs in beef stock and red wine gives them an even richer, meatier flavour, while making an incredible sauce to serve them with at the same time. If duck isn't your thing, you can use this same exact braise recipe for short ribs, pork shoulder, pig's head, veal breast or chicken legs (switch the beef stock for chicken stock in that case).

SERVES 4

4 large whole duck legs, trimmed of excess fat

½ teaspoon salt

freshly ground black pepper

1 teaspoon Chinese five-spice powder

1 tablespoon olive oil

6 garlic cloves, chopped

3 shallots, chopped

1 large onion, chopped

6 sprigs thyme

6 sprigs rosemary

2 bay leaves

500ml red wine

1.9 litres low-sodium beef stock

360ml orange juice

1. Pat the duck legs dry with kitchen paper and sprinkle them with the salt and pepper to taste and the five-spice powder.

2. In a Dutch oven large enough to fit the duck legs in a single layer, heat the oil over a medium-high heat until it shimmers. Add the duck legs skin-side down and cook without touching them until the skin is deep golden brown and crisp, about 15 minutes. Turn the legs over and cook them for a further 2 minutes, then remove them to a plate.

3. Preheat the oven to 160°C/gas mark 3.

4. Add the garlic, shallots and onion to the Dutch oven and cook over a medium heat until softened, about 5 minutes. Add the thyme, rosemary and bay leaves and cook, stirring, for a further 3 minutes. Pour off all but 2 tablespoons of the fat.

5. Add the wine and bring to the boil, scraping up the lovely browned bits that will have stuck to the bottom of the pan. Continue to boil the mixture until reduced by half, about 10 minutes. Return the duck legs to the pan, skin side up, and add the stock and orange juice. Bring the liquid to the simmer, cover the pan, and transfer it to the oven. After 20 minutes, reduce the temperature to 150°C/gas mark 2. Cook for 45 minutes, then check the liquid level; if it's beginning to dry out, top it up with beef stock until the duck legs are more than halfway submerged. Braise until very tender, about 1 further hour.

6. Transfer the duck legs to a plate and, if there's lots of excess fat on the surface of the cooking liquid, remove some with a spoon. Strain the liquid through a fine-mesh sieve, rinse out the Dutch oven and return the cooking liquid back to the pan, pressing hard on the solids to extract all the delicious liquid. Boil the pan sauce until it's reduced by one third and slightly thickened, about 10 minutes. Serve the duck legs drizzled with pan sauce.

GRILLED ASPARAGUS WITH FRIED DUCK EGGS

I don't cook at home as much as you might think, just like I'm sure a carpenter doesn't rush home from work to build himself a new shed. I did, however, go and buy a spiffy grill for the garden that features a double burner on the side, on the premise that if I'm going to be cooking on my own time, I might as well be outdoors as much as possible while I'm doing it. For a recipe like this one, which includes a mix of hob and grill cooking, a grill like mine saves a lot of running about.

Duck eggs are colossal compared with the hen eggs we're all used to, with gorgeous, fatty, rich yolks. Do make a reasonable effort to find them (in most supermarkets, for instance), as they're pretty spectacular. They're key to setting this dish apart, as is the duck prosciutto – which I'm sure you all started on six weeks ago, right? Of course, if need be, hen eggs and shop-bought prosciutto or country ham can be substituted and the whole thing will still be delicious.

SERVES 4

2 large bunches very thick green asparagus (16 spears total)

1 tablespoon olive oil, plus more for drizzling

1 garlic clove, finely chopped

sea salt

30g unsalted butter

8 fresh duck eggs (chicken eggs may be substituted)

115g freshly grated Parmesan

16–20 paper-thin slices Duck Prosciutto (page 96; regular prosciutto may be substituted)

freshly ground black pepper

¼ lemon

1. Light your grill for medium-high-heat cooking. Snap off and discard the woody bases from the asparagus. In a large bowl, toss the asparagus with the oil, garlic and salt to taste. Make sure you rub the oil onto the asparagus evenly.

2. Cook the asparagus on the grill with the lid down for 5 minutes, turning it just once; we want some char marks from the grill bars to help cut the richness of the eggs and cheese.

3. Heat a large cast-iron or non-stick pan over a medium-high heat, add the butter and wait until it begins to foam. Add the eggs to the hot butter four at a time and sprinkle them with salt and pepper. Cook them until the whites are opaque but the yolks are still runny. Remove the eggs to kitchen paper and cook the second batch.

4. Remove the asparagus from the grill and either divide it among four plates or plate the whole lot. Sprinkle the asparagus with Parmesan and lay the fried eggs on top. Sprinkle more Parmesan, followed by the duck prosciutto and a last layer of Parmesan. Drizzle the dish with oil, add a dash of salt, a grind of pepper and a squeeze of lemon juice.

THE PIG

PORK AND BEEF WERE THE MOST POPULAR MEATS IN THE UK UNTIL 2014 when they were eclipsed by chicken. If you care to thumb through the index of this book, you can see where my loyalties lie. One chicken recipe; three for beef; for pork, nine.

Such is my love for all parts of the pig that I could write a whole book on pork, but I've somehow managed to restrain myself and start you lads off with just a few really solid recipes, the crème de la crème of my pig dossier – including a mind-blowingly tender slow-cooked pork shoulder and a salty-sweet rack of grilled pork ribs that will leave you saying, 'Cow, who?'

PRESSURE COOKER CASSOULET

At my restaurants, we have always cooked our dried beans in a pressure cooker because it makes them super tender, and they don't burst through their skins the way they sometimes can when you boil them in water. That got me thinking about making cassoulet – that hearty winter stew of beans and pork from the southwest of France – in the same fashion. This recipe gets you all the same gloriously rich flavours of a slow-cooked cassoulet, only it won't take you all day.

SERVES 4

3 tablespoons blended vegetable oil

675g pork shoulder, cut into 2.5cm cubes

coarse sea salt and freshly ground black pepper

2 × 115g pork sausages (any kind will do, but preferably raw)

140g unsalted butter

1 large yellow onion, diced

3 garlic cloves

2 sprigs thyme

1 sprig rosemary

2 bay leaves

1 tablespoon fennel seeds

1 tablespoon tomato purée

5 vine ripened tomatoes, peeled and chopped

360ml white wine

4 drops Tabasco sauce

5 tablespoons Worcestershire sauce

170g dried white beans (such as cannellini, flageolet or haricot), soaked overnight in cold water to cover by a few centimetres

950ml chicken stock

2 tablespoons fines herbes (equal parts tarragon, chervil, and chives), roughly chopped

1. Heat the oil in a pressure cooker set over a high heat. Season the pork shoulder well and sear it until browned on all sides, 5–7 minutes. Remove the meat to a plate and sear the sausages on all sides, about 5 minutes. Remove them as well.

2. Reduce the heat to medium and add half of the butter. When it starts to foam, add the onion, garlic, thyme, rosemary, bay leaves and fennel seeds. Sweat the herbs and veg until soft and fragrant. Add the tomato purée and cook, stirring, for 1 minute.

3. Stir in the chopped tomatoes followed by the wine, using a wooden spoon or spatula to scrape the browned bits from the bottom of the pan. Let the wine simmer and reduce until almost dry, 10–15 minutes.

4. Add the Tabasco sauce, Worcestershire sauce and remaining butter. Return the pork and sausages to the pressure cooker. Add the beans and chicken stock. Bring it to the boil and close the lid on the pressure cooker according to manufacturer's instructions.

5. Place the cooker under high pressure according to the manufacturer's instructions and cook for 45 minutes. Depressurise the cooker, remove the lid and stir through the fines herbes. Serve immediately.

CHARCUTERIE:
HOW TO ASSEMBLE THE ULTIMATE MEAT BOARD

I've loved charcuterie from the moment I could chew. The English excel at all manner of potted meats, sausages, terrines and bacon of course, and I was blessed to have an Italian aunt who would go to Italy every summer and return to England with mortadella, prosciutto and salami in tow, all of which I devoured with abandon.

I've worked at mastering the dark art of charcuterie ever since I started cooking as a teenager, and twenty-plus years later, I'm still learning. Curing meat is an intense, technical and time-consuming process, hard for even restaurants to get right. With all the phenomenal artisan charcuterie outfits out there today, I can't say that I recommend making your own at home. But one of the more underappreciated facets of being a good cook is becoming a discerning shopper. There is an art to putting together the ultimate selection of meats, which I'll endeavour to pass on to you here.

The term *charcuterie* encompasses all preserved meats, most of which came about as peasant dishes aimed at using up the uglier bits of animals, turning scraps and odd cuts into something very delicious as well as long-lasting. These days, of course, terrines, pâtés, cured meats and the like are treated as luxury foods. A good charcuterie spread is a beautiful thing to behold; a pure and simple pleasure delivery system.

First, let's survey the meatscape. Charcuterie goes beyond prosciutto, lads! I divide it into the following categories:

- Dried salamis, such as Spanish chorizo, Italian soppressata and French saucisson sec

- Whole muscles, such as prosciutto, speck, coppa, bresaola, bacon and jamón ibérico

- Pâtés, terrines and mousses

- Smoked sausages, such as bratwurst or kielbasa

- Cold cooked sausages, such as mortadella

- Confit meat, such as potted meats or rillettes

Putting together a killer spread is all about balance. Try for a diversity of textures and flavours, working across the above categories as widely as possible. You'll want something spicy, something salty and something really fatty and unctuous. Try to represent a range of species too: pork, beef, duck, even rabbit and goose. Then you've got something for everyone, and you'll almost certainly introduce your mates to a delicious cut or preparation they've never tried before.

You may decide to really throw some weight behind the meat plate effort and make a terrine or mousse yourself, but for cured meats, you're best off leaving it to any one of a number of artisan charcuterie operations that have popped up all over the country.

If you're buying your meats over a counter, always ask to try a sample before you buy, since so much of what you select simply comes down to personal taste. A good rule of thumb, no matter what your preferences: if it's cheap, don't buy it.

How many types of meat you include depends upon how many people you're feeding. For a small group, a couple of salamis of different diameters, one or two pâtés and one or two whole muscles (like prosciutto, speck or bresaola) will do it, but the sky is the limit. At one point, at my restaurant Waterloo & City, we were serving a plate called 'The King' with twenty-five different types of house-made charcuterie on it. We had two guys working on our meats full-time, and they were curing and preserving anything that moved.

After you select your meats, then it's all about adding plenty of acid to balance all the fat and salt. Piccalilli, Branston pickle, savoury jams, Pickled Mustard Seeds (page 20), caper berries, cornichons, Tomato Confit (page 31) and Preserved Lemons (page 23) are all at home on a charcuterie board. And finally, I always offer both crisp biscuits and crusty sliced bread along with the meats.

Now, doesn't that feel like a hell of a lot of work, even if you haven't cooked a thing? Told you so.

THAI-SPICED PORK BELLY WITH FISH SAUCE CARAMEL

I'll admit that this dish is ridiculously labour-intensive for home cooking purposes, but it's so bloody delicious that I felt compelled to write the whole thing out for you anyway. It's a sort of homage to an incredible catfish dish that I ate at The Slanted Door, Charles Phan's Vietnamese restaurant in San Francisco. This is a pork belly version of that dish.

We always cook the pork belly using a technique that is a kind of poor man's *sous vide*. The idea is to wrap the belly in layer upon layer of clingfilm, followed by several layers of foil, and then roast it partially submerged in water. It's a cross between *sous vide* – the cooking method that involves vacuum sealing an ingredient and cooking it for very long periods submerged in warm water – and braising, where you roast something partly submerged in stock or wine. Braising dilutes the flavour of meat by letting its juices run out and be replaced by the wine or stock you're cooking it in; I find that meat cooked *sous vide* has a flat, gummy texture to it. This method improves on both, allowing the meat to almost confit in its own rendered fat and juices, keeping it tender and moist and maintaining a powerful flavour of pork.

At the very end, the pork belly bits get dunked in the fryer so they'll be crisp on the outside and pudding-soft on the inside, then lacquered with a salty-sweet fish sauce caramel.

SERVES 12 AS A NIBBLE

1 × 1.4–2.3kg skinless pork belly

240ml Thai-Spiced Pork Belly Rub (recipe follows)

cooking oil

240ml Fish Sauce Caramel (recipe follows)

1. Massage the pork belly thoroughly with the rub. Let it sit covered in the fridge for at least 24 and no more than 48 hours.

2. Give the pork a good wash and soak it under cold running water for 20–25 minutes. Pat it dry.

3. Pull a piece of clingfilm out onto a clean work surface and roll the pork belly in plastic no fewer than two or three times, keeping the belly as flat as possible. Turn the belly 180 degrees and wrap it in two or three more layers of plastic. Now repeat the process using foil. You'll end up with what looks like an enormous brick of cocaine.

4. Preheat the oven to 135°C/gas mark 1.

5. Place the pork belly packet in a large roasting tin and pour hot water in to reach halfway up the belly. Place the roasting tin on the hob and bring the water to the boil over a high heat. Carefully transfer the tin to the oven and cook it for 4 hours, topping up the water as necessary to keep it at around the same level. Remove it from oven and allow it to rest for 1 hour.

6. Remove the pork belly from the roasting tin to a high-sided baking sheet. Poke a few holes in the plastic and foil and drain off the juices (save and refrigerate them for later – beautiful on toast!). Unwrap the meat once it's cool enough to handle.

7. If you've got an electric fryer by chance, use it, because they're way safer; if not, use a heavy pan like a Dutch oven. Fill the fryer or pan half full with cooking oil. Position a thermometer in the oil and heat it nice and slow over a medium heat until the temperature reads 180°C.

8. Cut the pork belly into 5cm squares. Working a few pieces at a time, fry them until golden and crisp, 3–4 minutes. Remove them from the fryer to kitchen paper. Glaze with the fish sauce caramel either by brushing it on all sides or using a slotted spoon to submerge the pork belly in a bowl of the caramel. Eat immediately.

THAI-SPICED PORK BELLY RUB
MAKES 240ML

8 cloves

good pinch of fennel seeds

½ teaspoon coriander seeds

1 garlic clove

1 stalk lemongrass, peeled of its tough outer layers and sliced

100g coarse sea salt

1 teaspoon pink curing salt (also called Prague powder No. 2)

50g granulated sugar

pinch of smoked Spanish paprika

1 teaspoon Chinese five-spice powder

zest of 1 lemon, lime and orange

1. In a small frying pan over a medium-low heat, toast the cloves, fennel seeds and coriander seeds for a minute or two, until they begin to pop and turn fragrant. Grind them coarsely using a pestle and mortar or a spice grinder.

2. Add the garlic and lemongrass and break them down to a paste.

3. Add the salts, sugar, paprika, five-spice powder and citrus zests and mix well.

FISH SAUCE CARAMEL
MAKES 240ML

1 tablespoon rapeseed oil

¼ stalk lemongrass, peeled of its tough outer layers and thinly sliced

1 small garlic clove, finely chopped

½ shallot, finely diced

1 large Fresno chilli, deseeded and finely diced

½ tablespoon peeled finely diced ginger

1 teaspoon coriander seeds

200g granulated sugar

4 tablespoons Thai fish sauce

1 tablespoon rice wine vinegar

½ tablespoon fresh lemon juice

1 tablespoon chopped fresh coriander

1. Heat the rapeseed oil in a medium heavy-based saucepan set over a medium heat. Add the lemongrass, garlic, shallot, chilli, ginger and coriander seeds and cook for 5–10 minutes, until soft.

2. Add the sugar to the pan and let it melt and turn a medium amber colour, 5–10 minutes. Watch it closely, as it will go from clear to burnt in the blink of an eye.

3. As soon as the sugar is medium amber in colour, dump in the fish sauce and vinegar and bring to the boil – careful, it will spit and sputter. Stir to dissolve any lumps of caramel.

4. Allow the caramel to cool to room temperature, then add the lemon juice and coriander. Use it warm; it will keep in the fridge for at least a month.

SLOW-COOKED PORK SHOULDER

There's little that compares to the carnivorous pleasure of sinking your teeth into meltingly tender, salty, sweet, spicy slow-cooked pork. This is a recipe that we developed for a happy hour sandwich at Waterloo & City, and we literally couldn't cook enough of it to keep up with demand.

The paradox of big, heavily used muscles like leg and shoulder roasts of beef, lamb or pork is that the longer you cook them at low temperatures, the more tender they become. That's because they contain a lot of collagen, which melts in the heat and bastes and tenderises the muscle fibres while they cook; after 8 or 10 hours, you can pull apart a pork shoulder with only so much as a fork. These cuts are supremely low-maintenance, as you can pop them in the oven and forget about them without worrying that you'll overcook dinner. Keep in mind that cooking low and slow only works with collagen-rich meats – so don't try to do it with your Thanksgiving turkey, which will turn into a proper nightmare of scorched, tough flesh if left in the oven for a couple of extra hours.

SERVES 8–10

50g coarse sea salt

1½ tablespoons brown sugar

3 ½ tablespoons smoked Spanish paprika

1 tablespoon mustard powder

1 tablespoon onion powder

1 tablespoon garlic powder

1½ teaspoons chilli powder

1½ teaspoons ground cumin

1 × 2.7–3.6kg boneless pork shoulder (if using bone-in, add another hour to the cooking time)

Chuck the salt, brown sugar and spices into a small bowl and toss them together until evenly combined. Lay the pork shoulder on a clean work surface and pack it all over with the spice mixture, making sure to hit all the nooks and crevices. Transfer it to a ziplock bag or a sealed storage container and refrigerate it for no less than 8 hours, no more than 24 hours.

TO COOK IT IN THE OVEN:

1. Remove the pork shoulder from the fridge and allow it to come to room temperature, about 1 hour; preheat the oven to 120°C/gas mark ½ during the last 20 minutes.

2. Place the pork shoulder in a roasting tin fat-side up and pour about 1cm water into the tin. Roast until the meat's internal temperature reaches 74°C, 6–8 hours (for super-tender pulled pork, push it an hour or two further to 90°C). Add more water to the tin if it dries out during cooking. Remove the pork shoulder from the oven, cover with foil and let it rest for 30 minutes to catch the steam as it cools.

3. Slice the joint or pull the meat apart with a fork and serve.

TO COOK IT ON THE GRILL:

1. If you have a gas grill, light one side and preheat the grill to a temperature between 100 and 120°C (the lower the better). For a charcoal grill, light a pile of coals on one half of the grill and wait for the temperature to fall below 120°C. Meanwhile, remove the pork shoulder from the fridge and allow to come to room temperature, about 1 hour.

2. Place the pork shoulder fat-side up on the cool side of grill and position an aluminium tin filled with a few centimetres of water on the shelf above it; this will allow the pork shoulder to baste itself as it cooks. Doing your best to keep the grill temperature between 100°C and 120°C, cook the joint to an

internal temperature of at least 74°C. This can take anywhere from 6–12 hours, depending on the weight of the roast and the grill temperature; expect 90 minutes per 450g at 110°C. Add more water to the aluminium tin if it runs dry. Remove the pork shoulder from the grill, cover with foil to catch the steam as it cools, and let it rest for 30 minutes.

3. Slice the joint or pull the meat apart with a fork and serve.

DEAD-EASY PORK RIBS WITH PALM SUGAR GLAZE

Chinese five-spice powder is one of my all-time favourite seasonings, and I encourage you to get very friendly with it. It takes its name not from the number of ingredients, but the way this single spice mix hits on all five principal tastes (sweet, salty, sour, bitter and umami). The flavour is warm and sweet, and I find that it acts like a bridge between salt and the heat of chillies, giving these ribs a really round, warm deliciousness. It's a wonderful, versatile seasoning to add to pork, beef or duck. Chinese five-spice powder also lends meat a handsome reddish tone – like that nice red bark that you get when you put meat in a smoker – which is a big improvement over the unappetising gray tinge that ribs can take on when they're cooked in the oven.

SERVES 6

2 racks pork spare ribs cut St. Louis-style by your butcher

coarse sea salt and freshly ground black pepper

2 teaspoons Chinese five-spice powder

240ml Palm Sugar Caramel (recipe follows)

1. Preheat the oven to 110°C/ gas mark ¼.

2. Season your ribs on both sides very simply with salt and pepper and dust with the Chinese five-spice powder.

3. Place the ribs meat-side down in a pair of aluminium or glass baking dishes. Cover the dishes with foil and roast the meat for 4 hours.

4. Drain off the drippings. Flip the ribs over using two spatulas (and an extra pair of hands, if you have them) so the meat side is now up. Be gentle, as they may be so tender they start falling apart. Paint a layer of palm sugar caramel on the ribs and return them to the oven uncovered for a further 20–30 minutes. Serve straight out of the oven.

PALM SUGAR CARAMEL
MAKES ABOUT 360ML

400g palm sugar

1 tablespoon fresh lemon juice

200g thinly sliced shallots (from 4–6 large shallots)

1 dried hot red chilli, such as *chilli de árbol*

3 star anise

1 cinnamon stick

2 teaspoons freshly ground black pepper

120ml Thai fish sauce

1. In a heavy-based medium saucepan set over a medium heat, combine the palm sugar, lemon juice and 4 tablespoons water and bring the mixture to the boil. Using a wet pastry brush, wash down any sugar crystals that have stuck to the side of the pan. Reduce the heat to medium-low and let the mixture simmer undisturbed until it begins to reach a medium amber colour, about 20 minutes (watch the pan carefully, because caramel can go from pale to burnt in a matter of seconds).

2. Remove the saucepan from the heat and stir in the shallots, chilli, star anise, cinnamon and black pepper. Carefully whisk in the fish sauce and another 4 tablespoons water – the caramel will seize up and spit. Return the pan to a medium heat and stir it until the caramel is smooth and dissolved. Pour it into a heatproof bowl and let it cool completely. Remove the chilli, star anise and cinnamon stick and use while warm.

ROASTED PIG'S HEAD

Admittedly, a severed head doesn't scream 'delicious' (technically it doesn't scream anything – ha, ha!). The first time I saw my granddad roast a pig's head, I honestly assumed that it was for the dog, and I felt sorry for the poor bastard. But once I got a taste of the crisp skin, melt-in-your-mouth jowls, tongue, cheeks and even a bit of creamy brain served with mashed potatoes and applesauce, I have to admit that I became a twelve-year-old believer. So man up and have a go! Brining really helps to take away the livery tang that you get with cuts like these, so I'm doing you a favour here that granddad never did for me.

SERVES 2–3

1 whole pig's head, split (Either have your butcher do the honours, or do it at home with a wood saw. I've tried a chainsaw and it's too messy, lads.)

3.8 litres Pork Brine (recipe follows)

1 small carrot, finely chopped

½ onion, finely chopped

1 leek, white part only, finely chopped

3 sticks celery, finely chopped

1. First things first: pig heads come hairy, so you've either got to give this puppy a shave or blowtorch the hair off him. Burning hair stinks to high heaven, so I recommend going the Gillette route. No shaving cream necessary.

2. Brining time! In two ziplock bags or large containers of some description, submerge each half of the head in the pork brine. Refrigerate them for at least 24 hours and no more than 5 days.

3. Time for a wash! Put the head in the sink inside a bowl of clean cold water and let the tap run on top to keep circulating fresh cold water. The longer the brine, the longer the wash – 15 minutes per 24 hours is a good guideline.

4. Preheat the oven to 150°C/gas mark 2.

5. Pull a piece of clingfilm out onto a clean work surface and roll one of the head halves in plastic no fewer than two or three times. Turn it 180 degrees and wrap it in two or three more layers of plastic. Now do the same thing with foil. Repeat the process for the other half.

6. Place both head halves flat-sides down in a large roasting tin and pour hot water in to reach halfway up them. Place the roasting tin on the hob and bring the water to the boil over a high heat. Carefully transfer the tin to the oven and cook for 4 hours, topping up the water as necessary to keep it at around the same level. Remove the roasting tin from the oven and allow it to rest for 30 minutes.

7. Turn your oven temperature up to 190°C/gas mark 5. Spread the chopped vegetables evenly on a fresh roasting tin or baking sheet, unwrap the head halves, and arrange them flat-side down on top of the vegetables. Roast until the skin is golden and crisp, 45–60 minutes.

8. Serve the head (and vegetables, if you fancy) with mashed potatoes and applesauce. Everything in the head but the bones is edible, so dig in.

PORK BRINE
MAKES 3.8 LITRES

3.8 litres water

200g coarse sea salt

100g brown sugar

20g coriander seeds

3 tablespoons black peppercorns

2 tablespoons cloves

6 bay leaves

8 garlic cloves

1 lemon peel

1 orange peel

4 star anise

1 cinnamon stick

1 bunch coriander stems

20g dried whole chillies, such
as *chillies de árbol*

Combine all the ingredients in a large stockpot
and bring to the boil over a high heat. Reduce the
heat to medium and let the mixture simmer for
10 minutes, then remove it from the heat, cool
completely, and chill it down fridge-cold before
using.

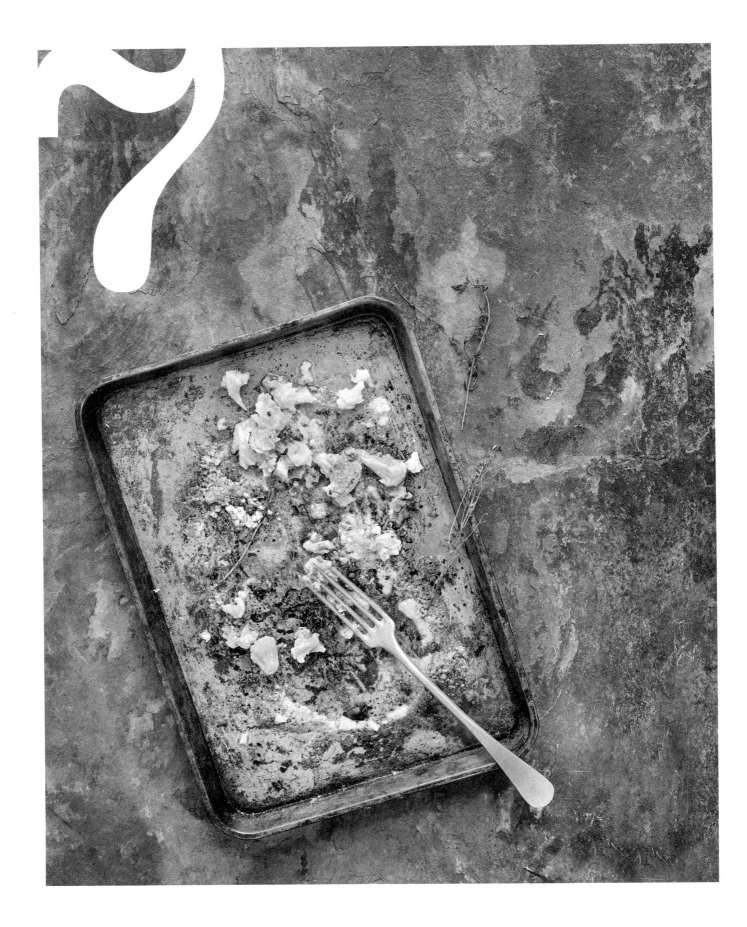

VEG

IF THERE'S ONE MALE STEREOTYPE I'M EAGER TO PUT TO REST, it's the one that says we're all Neanderthals interested in cooking and eating only meat. Yes, meat is easy to love, but I know plenty of blokes who appreciate a ripe local tomato with a little sea salt and olive oil or root vegetables roasted golden and sweet. Including me.

Unlike meat, most vegetables on their own don't have much in the way of umami: that rich, savoury flavour that makes food taste substantial. Learning to prepare them to maximise their depth of flavour – browning or grilling them, for instance, or complementing them with ingredients like cheese, vinegar or oil – is key to making them really shine. What follows is a rock-solid selection of veg options for every time of year, from evergreen dishes like Caesar salad and roasted cauliflower to a salt-baked corn on the cob that's unbeatable at the height of summer.

ROCKET SALAD WITH SMOKED ALMONDS AND CRISPY SHALLOTS

Right lads, salad time: this one doesn't feel like diet food thanks to the Parmesan and bits of fried shallot sprinkled throughout (far fresher versions of those atrociously unhealthy but totally addictive crispy fried onion rings). If you're pressed for time, you can skip the shallots and you've got a salad that comes together in under fifteen minutes and still has plenty of flavour and texture to spare from the almonds, cheese and rock-solid balsamic vinaigrette.

SERVES 4–6

4 large shallots, peeled

240ml whole milk

rapeseed oil for frying

260g plain flour (use '00' flour for extra-crispy shallots)

sea salt for seasoning shallots

225g wild rocket (about 4 big handfuls)

200–250g smoked almonds

100g grated Parmesan

Balsamic Vinaigrette (page 126)

sea salt and freshly ground black pepper

1. Shave the shallots very thinly with a Japanese mandoline or sharp knife; separate the rings. Soak the shallots in the milk for at least 30 minutes to remove some of their sharpness.

2. Fill a Dutch oven or other heavy-based pan with 5–7.5cm oil. Position a thermometer in the oil and heat it nice and slow over a medium heat until the temperature reads 180°C.

3. Drain the shallots well, then toss them in flour (this is called dredging). Bounce them around in a metal sieve for a bit to shake the excess flour off. Place the shallots in the oil, stirring them constantly with a slotted spoon and making sure they don't stick together, until golden brown, 1–2 minutes. Using a slotted spoon, remove them to a kitchen paper-lined baking sheet to absorb the excess grease. Season with salt while hot. Allow them to cool and use them immediately, or store them in an airtight container for up to 2 days.

4. Wash the rocket and chuck it in a large bowl. Sprinkle the smoked almonds, fried shallots and Parmesan over the top. Drizzle your dressing around the edges of the bowl, and in a clockwise motion, turn the salad until all the leaves and garnishes are evenly dressed. Taste your salad and season with salt and pepper as needed – that's right, salad needs a touch of salt just like everything else!

BUTTERHEAD LETTUCE SALAD WITH HONEY MUSTARD DRESSING

The thing about salads is that we know we're supposed to be eating them, but the fancy versions you find in so many cookery books and restaurants these days are bitter and sour and not very pleasant to eat. This is a good, honest salad without all the weird bells and whistles – just sweet, delicious butterhead lettuce. Let's not kid ourselves: there is very little nutritional value in lettuce, but it's the perfect vehicle to transport oil, vinegar and mustard, all of which are good for our stomachs and livers.

SERVES 2

FOR THE SALAD DRESSING:

1 garlic clove, peeled and sliced in half

1 tablespoon Dijon mustard

1 tablespoon honey

3 tablespoons white wine vinegar

sea salt and freshly ground black pepper

240ml extra-virgin olive oil

FOR THE SALAD:

1 butterhead lettuce (organic/hydroponic is best, but don't beat yourself up about it)

1 shallot, thinly sliced (optional)

30g croutons (see Note) (optional)

leaves from ½ bunch flat-leaf parsley (optional)

4 breakfast radishes, sliced (optional)

1. Make the dressing: get out a small bowl and rub the sides with garlic, then toss out the spent clove. Whisk together the mustard, honey, vinegar and salt and pepper to taste for a minute (be sure to add the salt at this stage, because it won't dissolve once the oil is added). Add the oil in a slow, constant stream, whisking all the while. Transfer the dressing to a bottle or mason jar.

2. Make the salad: give your lettuce a quick rinse under cold water, then tear the leaves down into manageable pieces. Toss those in a big bowl along with whatever garnishes you're using: I suggest shallots, croutons, parsley and radishes, but don't limit yourself. Drizzle your dressing around the edges of the bowl, never directly onto the leaves, as it will puddle up in the lettuce and you'll end up with an uneven distribution of dressing. In a clockwise motion, turn the salad until all the leaves and garnishes are evenly dressed. Season with salt and pepper.

3. Serve immediately; the moment the vinegar hits those leaves they start to go limp, and nobody likes a limp salad.

Note: To make croutons: Preheat the oven to 160°C/gas mark 3. Cut the crust off any bread and slice it into 2.5cm cubes. Figure on 15g of bread cubes per person. Toss the cubes in just enough oil to lightly coat them and spread them in a single layer on a baking sheet. Bake them until golden brown and crisp throughout, anywhere from 5–15 minutes depending on the size of your cubes. Use them immediately.

CAESAR SALAD

In my first year of cooking school we were sent out to do a work placement in a local professional kitchen. I was lucky enough to be sent to one of the better restaurants in Nottingham and was subsequently opened up to cuisine that was very different from the meat and potatoes I was used to: things like roast duck, fresh tuna and Caesar salad. Caesar salad seems a bit old-fashioned these days, but it was avant-garde stuff in the north of England in the early 90s.

The Caesar is aptly named, because it truly is the king of salads; I don't care whether or not it's considered trendy these days. Keep in mind that the salad itself is basically just a delivery mechanism for the dressing, so whatever you do, don't 'cheat' with a shop-bought version. Dress it with oil and vinegar before you do that.

SERVES 4

1 loaf sourdough bread for croutons

extra virgin olive oil

2 hearts of cos lettuce, large outer leaves removed

4 large eggs

sea salt and freshly ground black pepper

100g grated Parmesan

2 tablespoons chopped fresh chives

240ml Caesar Dressing (recipe follows)

4 marinated Spanish white anchovies

1. Preheat the oven to 160°C/gas mark 3.

2. First, make the croutons: cut the crust off the bread and slice it into roughly 1cm cubes. Toss them in just enough oil to lightly coat and spread them in a single layer on a baking sheet. Bake until golden brown and crisp throughout, about 10 minutes depending on the exact size of your cubes. Let them cool.

3. Dice the cos leaves or slice them into strips, being careful to avoid the core at the bottom of the heart.

4. Heat a splash of oil in a cast-iron or Teflon frying pan over a medium-high heat and fry each egg until the whites are opaque but the yolks are still runny; season with salt and pepper while they cook. Hold them in a warm place while you dress your salad.

5. In a medium bowl, combine the lettuce, 70g of the Parmesan, the croutons, chives and one quarter of the dressing to start off. Mix well, taste and add more dressing as desired. Season with salt and pepper.

6. Divide the salad among plates or bowls and top with a fried egg, white anchovy and more Parmesan.

CAESAR DRESSING

MAKES 480ML

½ garlic clove
1 salted anchovy fillet
2 teaspoons white wine vinegar
1½ teaspoons Worcestershire sauce
1 teaspoon Dijon mustard
drop of Tabasco sauce
50g grated Parmesan
1 medium egg yolk
240ml blended vegetable oil
4 teaspoons warm water
sea salt and freshly ground black pepper

1. Chuck the garlic, anchovy, vinegar, Worcestershire sauce, mustard and Tabasco into a blender and purée until smooth.

2. Scrape the purée into a food processor and add the Parmesan and egg yolk. Blend for 1 minute. While the machine is running, add the oil in a slow, steady stream. As the dressing begins to thicken, alternate the stream of oil with teaspoons of warm water to keep the dressing from getting too thick and separating. Season with salt and pepper; use immediately or refrigerate for up to 3 days.

SOME VINAIGRETTES

Any salad dressing that you make yourself is going to be better than shop-bought ones designed to sit on a shelf for eons, so why overpay for a pretty label on a bottle full of chemicals and stabilisers? Roll up your sleeves and make your own. It needn't be complicated.

There are two basic types of vinaigrettes: emulsified and broken. Emulsified vinaigrettes tend to be three parts oil to one part vinegar and often use mustard or egg yolk to help the oil and vinegar blend and stay together. They are opaque, thick and creamy, and therefore best for sturdy lettuces like iceberg or cos that can stand up to a dressing with a lot of body. Broken vinaigrettes are usually equal parts oil and vinegar. While the two elements never fully combine as in an emulsified version, shaking them up just before use intersperses the oil and vinegar in little droplets. Broken vinaigrettes are thin and runny, which makes them perfect for delicate lettuces like round, rocket, or young leaves.

The acidity of these vinaigrettes keeps them from going off, so they'll stay good to use in your fridge until they're finished.

FRENCH VINAIGRETTE

MAKES 720ML

120ml Dijon mustard

120ml white wine vinegar

1¼ teaspoons sea salt, plus more if needed

8 turns of the pepper mill

480ml rapeseed or blended vegetable oil

In a medium bowl, combine the mustard, vinegar, salt and pepper. Whisk the vinegar mixture while slowly drizzling in the oil. Taste and add more salt if needed.

SHERRY VINAIGRETTE

MAKES ABOUT 480ML

1½ teaspoons Dijon mustard

4 tablespoons sherry vinegar

2½ tablespoons red wine vinegar

2 tablespoons water

2 tablespoons fresh lemon juice

½ garlic clove, grated on a Microplane

1 shallot, finely diced

1 teaspoon salt, plus more if needed

5 turns of the pepper mill

300ml rapeseed or blended vegetable oil

1. In a medium bowl, combine everything but the oil.

2. Whisk the vinegar mixture while slowly drizzling in the oil. For an emulsified vinaigrette, use a handheld blender instead of a whisk. Either way, shake the dressing well just before use. Taste and add more salt if needed.

(continued)

TRUFFLE VINAIGRETTE

MAKES ABOUT 600ML

½ garlic clove, grated on a Microplane

¼ shallot, finely diced

½ tablespoon grainy mustard

4 tablespoons Banyuls vinegar

1 tablespoon red wine vinegar

juice of ½ lemon

¼ cup truffle juice

1 teaspoon sea salt, plus more if needed

5 turns of the pepper mill

2 tablespoons black or white truffle oil

2 cups rapeseed or blended vegetable oil

40g tinned truffle peelings, or fresh black truffle, finely chopped

1. In a medium bowl, combine the garlic, shallot, mustard, vinegars, lemon juice, truffle juice, salt and pepper.

2. Whisk the vinegar mixture while slowly drizzling in the oils. For an emulsified vinaigrette, use a handheld blender instead of a whisk. Once all the oil is incorporated, mix in the truffle peelings. Taste and add more salt if needed.

RED WINE VINAIGRETTE

MAKES ABOUT 480ML

4 tablespoons red wine

1½ teaspoons Dijon mustard

4 tablespoons Cabernet Sauvignon vinegar or other good red wine vinegar

2 tablespoons fresh lemon juice

¼ garlic clove, grated on a Microplane

½ shallot, finely diced

1 teaspoon coarse sea salt, plus more if needed

6 turns of the pepper mill

300ml rapeseed or blended vegetable oil

1. In a small saucepan over a medium-high heat, reduce the wine by half, about 5 minutes.

2. In a medium bowl, combine the reduced wine, mustard, vinegar, lemon juice, garlic, shallot, salt and pepper. Whisk the vinegar mixture while slowly drizzling in the oil. Taste and add more salt if needed.

BALSAMIC VINAIGRETTE

MAKES 540–600ML

120ml good balsamic vinegar

4 tablespoons red wine vinegar

juice of ½ lemon

½ teaspoon Dijon mustard

2½ teaspoons coarse sea salt

10 turns of the pepper mill

55g seasonal fruit such as plums, figs, or apricots, finely chopped (optional)

360ml rapeseed or blended vegetable oil

Place all the ingredients except the oil in a medium bowl. Using a whisk or hand blender, slowly drizzle the oil into the vinegar base. Thin it with a touch of water if the dressing gets too thick.

BLANCHED PEAS WITH MINT, RICOTTA AND TOASTED WALNUTS

I have a massive love of springtime thanks to my upbringing in England, where the winters are long, wet, dark, cold, wet, gray, dreary – and did I mention wet? But all that horrible winter damp and mist makes Britain a gloriously green place in the spring and summer, full of colourful local produce to cook with. Peas, even though they're a pain in the arse to shell, have always been a favourite of mine.

The thing about peas is that they have a very short growing season, and all of their sweetness turns to mealy, bland starch within a couple days of being picked. This means that unless you can locate very fresh spring peas from a good farmers' market or home garden, you're actually best buying frozen ones. They are flash-frozen at their peak and therefore tend to be of a better quality, frankly, than all but the freshest spring peas.

SERVES 4–6

230g fresh or frozen English peas

115g walnuts, preferably whole

8 fresh mint leaves

2 shallots, finely chopped

small handful of fresh coriander leaves, chopped

sea salt and freshly ground black pepper

3–4 tablespoons Balsamic Vinaigrette (page 126)

225g Homemade Ricotta (page 62)

6–8 slices Ciabatta (page 49, or shop-bought), toasted

1. Preheat the oven to 160°C/gas mark 3.

2. If you're using fresh peas, bring a medium pan full of seawater-salty water to the boil and toss the peas in. Boil them for 6–8 minutes, then drain off the hot water and immediately transfer them to a bowl full of ice water to cool. If you're using frozen peas, allow them to thaw under cold running water.

3. Spread the walnuts evenly on a baking sheet, place them in the oven and toast until golden and fragrant, about 5 minutes, tossing them once to help them toast evenly. Transfer them to a plate to cool. Meanwhile, slice the mint into thin strips (this is called julienning).

4. Chuck the peas, walnuts, shallots, mint and coriander into a bowl and season with salt and pepper. Drizzle on as much vinaigrette as you like and toss the mixture to coat.

5. Transfer the pea salad to a serving bowl or plate and dollop the ricotta on top. Serve with ciabatta on the side.

ROASTED BABY ARTICHOKES WITH BACON AND BALSAMIC VINEGAR

For the past fifteen years or so, it seems like every restaurant in the western hemisphere has had Brussels sprouts, bacon and balsamic vinegar on its menu, and I'm guilty of it too. But it's with good reason: the dish is seriously tasty. When I opened my new Hollywood restaurant, Birch, I wanted to do something equally as delicious but a little bit different. So I substituted baby artichokes, in season in the spring and summer, to freshen up a wintry dish for the warmer months. Baby artichokes have the same earthiness as Brussels sprouts, but with a unique, sweet nuttiness too.

SERVES 4–6

9 baby artichokes (about 900g)

2 lemons, cut in half

225g thick-cut bacon, cut into 1cm lardons

1 teaspoon chopped fresh rosemary

2 garlic cloves, finely chopped

coarse sea salt

3 tablespoons good-quality balsamic vinegar

4 tablespoons extra virgin olive oil

¼ teaspoon flaky sea salt, such as Maldon

¼ teaspoon cracked black pepper

1. Prep each artichoke by removing the tough outer leaves and peeling the outer layer from the stem with a vegetable peeler or a paring knife. Cut off the top third of the artichoke to remove the tough ends of the leaves. Cut them in half lengthways and give them a rub all over with one of the lemons as you work so they don't oxidise and turn an unappealing brown colour.

2. Preheat the oven to 190°C/gas mark 5.

3. Place a frying pan big enough to fit the artichokes in a single layer over a medium heat. Add the bacon lardons and cook for 5 minutes, or until most of their fat has been rendered. Remove the bacon using a slotted spoon and set it aside on a plate.

4. Add the artichokes to the hot bacon fat in a single layer and let them brown, about 3 minutes. Transfer the pan to the oven and cook for 10 minutes, or until soft and tender.

5. Remove the pan from the oven and add the bacon back in, along with the rosemary and garlic. Return the pan to the hob over a medium heat. Give your best go at sautéing, tossing the ingredients around; if you drop some, don't worry, the dog will love you for it. Season with salt.

6. Add the vinegar to deglaze the pan, scraping up any browned bits with a wooden spoon, and let the vinegar reduce until sticky but not burnt, about 1 minute.

7. Transfer the artichokes and bacon to a serving bowl, drizzle with the oil and sprinkle with sea salt and pepper.

ROASTED WINTER VEGETABLE AND BURRATA SALAD

The idea of a warm salad sounds a bit daft, but the contrast of temperatures at play here is really quite delicious. This salad is all about a balance of diverse flavours and textures. The rich nuts and cheese along with the sweet root vegetables make it quite substantial and filling as salads go.

SERVES 4–6

115g hazelnuts

1 small parsnip

1 carrot

2 small turnips

4 small shallots

sea salt and freshly ground black pepper

120ml good-quality extra virgin olive oil, plus a bit more for the vegetables

4 tablespoons honey, preferably sage blossom honey

1 tablespoon Dijon mustard

4 tablespoons aged sherry vinegar

240ml grapeseed oil

1 chicory

1 red chicory

4 × 125g balls burrata cheese

1. Preheat the oven to 160°C/gas mark 3.

2. Spread the hazelnuts evenly on a baking sheet and toast them until golden brown and extremely fragrant, about 5 minutes. Crush them up a bit and set them aside.

3. Peel the parsnip, carrot, turnips and shallots and cut them into bite-size, roughly uniform pieces. Toss them in a bowl with salt, pepper and a touch of olive oil, then spread them evenly on a baking sheet and roast until soft and caramelised, about 25 minutes. Allow them to cool slightly.

4. While your vegetables are cooking, prepare the vinaigrette by whisking the honey, mustard and vinegar in a medium bowl. Add ½ teaspoon salt and 5 turns of the pepper mill. Slowly whisk in the grapeseed oil and the remaining olive oil.

5. In a large bowl, separate the chicory leaves and discard the cores. Add the roasted vegetables and half of the hazelnuts. Drizzle on as much vinaigrette as you like and toss to dress.

6. Divide the salad among plates or arrange it on a large serving plate. Break up the balls of burrata and distribute them across the top of the salad. Sprinkle the remaining hazelnuts on top and serve.

BEETROOT FROM A PRESSURE COOKER

I started cooking beetroot in a pressure cooker because I noticed that with light-coloured varieties like golden beetroot or candy-striped Chioggias, roasting them in the oven altered their colour for the worse. In a pressure cooker, not only do they keep their bright appearance, but they also cook much more quickly and keep their integrity better. So this one's a no-brainer.

SERVES 2

1 bunch beetroot (red, golden or Chioggia), scrubbed and tops removed

3 tablespoons extra virgin olive oil, plus more for finishing

coarse sea salt and freshly ground black pepper

1. Place the cleaned beetroot in a small bowl, toss them with the oil, and season with salt and pepper.

2. Pour 950ml water into your pressure cooker, insert a steamer tray, and place the dressed beetroot on top.

3. Close and lock the pressure cooker according to the manufacturer's instructions. Bring it to high pressure and cook the beetroot for 30 minutes. Depressurise the cooker and remove the beetroot. Allow them to cool and then, using kitchen paper or a paring knife, carefully peel off the skin.

4. Cut the beetroot into segments and dress them with some more oil, salt and pepper. Serve at room temperature.

JERUSALEM ARTICHOKE SOUP

Jerusalem artichokes – also known as sunchokes – have a sweet and nutty flavour that's unique in the vegetable world. At one of my first jobs, at a very famous restaurant in London, we made croquettes with sunchokes and I forgot to order them as part of our vegetable delivery. The sous chef, who I think wanted to fire me anyway, tossed me out on the street and told me to come back with sunchokes – not an easy find in London in the 90s – or lose my job. I spent hours walking around with the fear of God in me, and just when I'd almost given up, I stumbled across some at a market. Needless to say, I had a huge 'Go F yourself!' smile on my face when I handed them over.

These little tubers are just now gaining the popularity they deserve among chefs, who thanks to today's emphasis on cooking with the seasons find themselves scratching around for new and interesting flavours on their winter menus. Sunchokes are often served roasted, but I like them puréed smooth into soup and garnished with mushrooms (for umami) and smoked almonds (for texture).

SERVES 6

120ml extra virgin olive oil, plus more for drizzling

2 garlic cloves, finely chopped

1 teaspoon fresh thyme leaves, plus more for garnish

675g Jerusalem artichokes, peeled and chopped

700–950ml chicken stock

1 teaspoon coarse sea salt

¼ teaspoon freshly ground pepper

170g chanterelle mushrooms

2 teaspoons fresh lemon juice

5 tablespoons crème fraîche (optional)

25g chopped smoked almonds

1. Heat 2 tablespoons of the oil in a medium saucepan over a medium heat until it shimmers. Add the garlic and thyme and cook, stirring, for 1 minute.

2. Add the Jerusalem artichokes, 700ml of the chicken stock, 4 tablespoons of the remaining oil, the salt and pepper. Bring the liquid to a simmer and cover the pan. Reduce the heat to low and cook for 30 minutes, or until the artichokes are soft and are practically falling apart. If some of the tubers refuse to fall apart, cut them into smaller chunks with a knife (if you're in a terrible hurry, you can do this step in a pressure cooker at high pressure for 8–10 minutes).

3. Meanwhile, heat the remaining 2 tablespoons of oil in a medium sauté pan over a medium heat until it shimmers. Add the chanterelles and cook until golden, 4–5 minutes. Set them aside.

4. Dump the soup into a blender and purée it until silky smooth, adding up to a further 250ml of chicken stock to get it to your preferred texture. Stir in the lemon juice and half of the crème fraîche, if using.

5. Ladle the soup into bowls and top with the sautéed chanterelles, smoked almonds, some thyme leaves, the remaining crème fraîche and a drizzle of oil.

CAULIFLOWER THREE WAYS

Kale and Brussels sprouts might be the trendy vegetables du jour, but for me it doesn't get any better than plain old horrendously unfashionable cauliflower. I fell in love with it when I went to see my grandma as a small child, and she cooked a dish that we Brits call cauliflower cheese: a gratin of sorts that she made with the best British cheddar and cauliflower that granddad grew in his garden.

Cauliflower is incredibly versatile, holds up to strong flavours and it's really inexpensive for the quantity of food you get out of it. You can get specimens of a reasonably good quality all over the place, not just in fancy grocery stores and farmers' markets. Here are three of my favourite uses for dear old cauliflower, but simply boiled with a bit of salt and butter works just fine too.

SERVES 4

ROASTED WHOLE

115g salted butter

1 head medium–large cauliflower, green stalks and outer leaves removed

½ teaspoon cumin seeds

1 whole garlic clove

1 sprig thyme

1 sprig rosemary

sea salt and freshly ground black pepper

½ lemon

1. Preheat the oven to 180°C/gas mark 4.

2. Grab a medium cast-iron pan and melt half of the butter over a medium-high heat. Add the cauliflower and let it caramelise all over, adjusting it as necessary so that all of its surfaces colour evenly without burning. Remove the cauliflower from the pan and add the remaining butter, the cumin seeds, garlic and herbs, spooning them evenly around the surface of the pan.

3. Add the cauliflower back to the pan and spoon the butter over the top a few times. Transfer to the oven and cook for 15 minutes, basting it with the butter every 3–4 minutes (or as often as you can be bothered).

4. Remove the cauliflower from the oven and give it one last butter baste. Sprinkle it with salt, pepper and lemon juice. Cut it into wedges and serve.

(continued)

SOUP

SERVES 4

85g unsalted butter

½ yellow onion, sliced

2 garlic cloves, finely chopped

¼ teaspoon ground cumin

1 small head cauliflower, green stalks and outer leaves removed, roughly chopped

coarse sea salt

500ml chicken or vegetable stock

120ml double cream

freshly ground black pepper

85g Parmesan, grated

1. Place a 6-litre saucepan or Dutch oven over a medium-high heat and melt the butter. Reduce the heat to medium-low and add the onion and garlic. Cook until the onions become translucent and begin to smell sweet, 6–7 minutes.

2. Stir in the cumin and cook for a minute or two. Chuck in the cauliflower and a big pinch of salt and cook for a further 3 minutes.

3. Add the stock and jack up the heat to bring it to the boil. Reduce the heat to keep the soup at a simmer for 5–7 minutes. Add the cream and simmer for 3 further minutes.

4. Using a food processor, standing blender or, better yet, a hand blender, purée the soup until it's smooth as a baby's bottom. Taste and add more salt if necessary. Reheat the soup and serve it sprinkled with freshly ground black pepper and Parmesan.

'T-BONE' STEAKS

SERVES 4

1 medium to large head cauliflower,
green stalks and outer leaves removed

Splash of rapeseed oil

coarse sea salt and freshly ground black pepper

115–170g blue cheese, crumbled

4 tablespoons Herb Butter (page 35)

80g dried breadcrumbs

1 tablespoon chopped fresh parsley

1. Preheat the oven to 180°C/gas mark 4.

2. Place the cauliflower stem-end down on your
   chopping board and slice off the rounded ends on
   the right and left-hand sides. Slice it into four
   cross-sections of even thickness.

3. Heat a cast-iron frying pan over a medium-high
   heat and add a splash of oil. Season the cauliflower
   steaks with salt. Unless you have a flipping huge
   pan or a very small cauliflower, this probably will
   require working in batches or using two pans: sear
   the steaks on one side for 3–4 minutes, until golden
   brown. Flip them and spread crumbled blue
   cheese and bits of the herb butter as evenly as
   possible on top. Sprinkle with breadcrumbs.

4. Transfer the pan to the oven and cook until the
   cauliflower is tender, the butter and cheese are
   melted, and breadcrumbs are golden and crisp,
   5–10 minutes. Repeat step 3 with the remaining
   cauliflower steaks as necessary. Sprinkle with
   freshly ground black pepper and parsley and serve.

THREE POTATO RECIPES

Growing up in England in the 1980s, pasta, rice and certainly any sort of Asian noodle or grains like quinoa or farro were seriously edgy stuff. I was raised on potatoes; ate them with practically every meal. A nice creamy mash or a stack of crispy chips to this day reminds me of the comforts of home.

When it comes to cooking potatoes, it's all about honing and perfecting a few versatile methods rather than trying out a bunch of crazy recipes; keep the potatoes uncomplicated and look to your veg for newness and variation. The following recipes relay my tried-and-tested techniques to boil, mash and fry potatoes – the only three preparations you need in order to round out any dinner plate, any time of the year.

PLAIN BOILED POTATOES

Beginner cooks have a nasty habit of either undercooking boiled potatoes or severely overcooking them. Undercooked spuds are crunchy and therefore more or less inedible, and when overcooked, they get waterlogged and taste of nothing. The key to getting them just right is timing, not water temperature. Let them boil away, then take them off the heat once a knife slides through the potatoes without any resistance, like a hot knife through butter. If the water becomes floury and the potatoes start to break apart, you've overcooked them. Start over.

Don't let the use of mint in this recipe throw you off. It has the effect of slightly sweetening the potatoes but won't leave them tasting like toothpaste or chewing gum.

SERVES 2

450g Charlotte or Anya potatoes
1 teaspoon coarse sea salt
3 sprigs mint
1 sprig thyme
8 black peppercorns
salted butter or Whipped Lardo (page 59), to serve

1. Give your potatoes a good scrub, put them in a large saucepan and cover them with water by at least 2.5cm. Add the salt and stir. Bring the water to the boil and add the mint, thyme and peppercorns.

2. Boil the potatoes until tender, 15–25 minutes, depending on their size. Turn off the heat and leave the potatoes to cool in the water. This will allow them to soak up the flavour of the herbs and pepper and keep them from steaming themselves dry.

3. Drain the potatoes and serve them with a knob of butter or perhaps a dollop of Whipped Lardo (especially if they're going with pork).

THE MOST EXCELLENT MASHED POTATOES

A great mashed potato recipe is one of the best things a man can learn. They go with nearly anything and good-quality potatoes are easy to find wherever you are in the world. My ideal mashed potatoes are glossy, custardy and contain almost as much butter as potato (sorry, but they're not a diet food). I like to use Yukon gold potatoes, because they have a buttery richness to them and don't absorb a lot of water when cooking.

Pick out potatoes that are even in size and don't have too many eyes (which are a sign that they're really old). If they've been sitting in your kitchen larder for a while, make sure they're still firm with a sweet – never musty – smell to them. Keep in mind that mashed potatoes don't make good leftovers, so cook only what you'll eat in one sitting. They absorb moisture and take on off flavours in the fridge, and once cooled and reheated, they'll never have the same texture again.

SERVES 6–8

sea salt

1 pound large Yukon Gold *or* Maris Piper potatoes, peeled and cut into quarters

about 450g unsalted butter

about 120ml organic whole milk

1. Bring 2 litres of water with 1 tablespoon salt to the boil over a high heat. Add the potatoes and cook for 12–15 minutes, until a paring knife can be easily inserted and removed from the potatoes.

2. Reduce the heat to low. Drain the potatoes well and return them to the pan for a minute or two to evaporate any excess water, stirring them constantly. Put the potatoes through a potato ricer.

3. In the same pan set over a medium heat, melt 340g of the butter and add 4 tablespoons milk. Add the potatoes and a pinch of salt and whisk the mixture together, continuing to add milk until the potatoes take on an almost custard-like consistency. At this stage, you can add more butter and salt to suit your taste, but it's important to maintain the earthy flavour of the potatoes – so don't get too greedy with the butter.

(continued)

TRIPLE-COOKED CHIPS

'Chips' in England are what Americans call 'fries' (to confuse matters further, US 'chips' are UK 'crisps'). Regardless of what the hell you call them, chips, crisps, hash browns, French fries, home fries, patatas bravas – fried potatoes of all sorts might be the most consumed snack in the Western world. My feeling is that if you're going to down this much fat and salt, they'd better be proper worth it. That's why I make the chips in-house at my restaurant instead of buying in the frozen kind, much as my overworked cooks would probably prefer to do the latter and save themselves a couple hours on spud duty every morning. Boiled, oven-dried, and twice fried, these chips end up with a mashed-potato-soft interior and a fried crust so sturdy that they crunch when you eat them.

SERVES 4

900g Maris Piper or russet potatoes
sea salt
rapeseed oil for frying

1. Scrub the potatoes under cold water. Using a sharp knife, square off their round edges slightly, then slice them 1.5cm thick.

2. Preheat the oven to 190°C/gas mark 5.

3. Chuck the chips in a pan and cover them with cold, seawater-salty water by at least 2.5cm. Bring the water to the simmer over a medium-high heat; it's important to always start potatoes cooking in cold water and heat them gradually, which allows them to release starch and prevents them from becoming gummy. Leave the potatoes to cook all the way through, 5 or so minutes after the water begins to simmer.

4. Line two baking sheets with greaseproof paper. Gently remove the potatoes from the hot water to one of the sheets and place them in the oven for 2 minutes to dry – this will help them crisp in the fryer and develop a really crunchy outside shell.

5. If you've got an electric fryer by chance, use it, because they're way safer; if not, take a heavy pan like a Dutch oven and fill it half full with oil. Position a thermometer in the oil and heat it nice and slow over a medium heat until the temperature reads 150°C.

6. Transfer the potatoes to the fryer in batches and fry them until pale golden, about 2 minutes. Remove them from the fryer with a slotted spoon or skimmer to the second parchment-lined baking sheet and place them back in the oven for a further 2 minutes. At this point, the chips can be cooled and stored in a sealed container in the fridge for a day or two.

7. Increase the oil temperature to 190°C and return the chips to the fryer once more, again working in batches. This time, cook them until deep golden and very crisp, 2–3 minutes. Remove them to kitchen paper and immediately hit them with salt. Serve immediately.

SPECIAL DAYS

A SUMMER BARBECUE

SPINACH AND ARTICHOKE DIP

LAMB BELLY WITH MINT SAUCE

CORN ON THE COB WITH CHILLI-LIME BUTTER

LAMBURGERS

ROOT VEGETABLES

SWORDFISH WITH SALSA VERDE

CHICKEN AL MATTONE

THE GRILLING RECIPES THAT I REGULARLY COME ACROSS IN COOKBOOKS are unbelievably one-dimensional and boring; basically, endless repetitions of the same steak and hamburger cuisine. Rather than pile on a few more, I thought I'd show you lads what your grills can really do. Think lamb belly and swordfish, not burgers and sausages. Pick and choose from the recipes in this chapter to create whatever sort of barbecue style suits your fancy.

SPINACH AND ARTICHOKE DIP

I know I've put artichokes in the title of this book, but if I'm being honest, I had never seen one, never mind eaten one until I was nineteen, and my first impression was, 'That's a lot of messing about for something so bland!' I still think they're a pain in the arse to prepare, but in season and with a lot of love, I now appreciate that artichokes are absolutely delicious and just about worth all the effort. I would recommend steering clear of the prepared tinned ones, tempting as they are, because they are flavourless and sometimes have a woody texture.

I wanted to include a recipe for artichoke dip for a couple of reasons: first, because we love dips. Second, because I think that other than being served with bacon and Balsamic Vinaigrette (page 126), this is the absolute best way to eat them.

SERVES 6

4 medium globe artichokes

1 whole garlic clove

1 slice lemon

1 bay leaf

sea salt

2 tablespoons extra virgin olive oil

3 garlic cloves, finely chopped

125g fresh baby spinach, chopped

225g ricotta cheese

225g cream cheese

1 teaspoon chilli flakes

1 tablespoon tahini

freshly ground black pepper

50g grated Parmesan

fresh lemon juice

Pitta Bread (page 157), to serve (optional)

1. Using a serrated knife, cut 2–2.5cm off the top of an artichoke. Pull off the scabby, smaller leaves toward the base and on the stem. Cut the stem back to 2.5cm in length. Repeat with the remaining artichokes.

2. Fill a large pan with 5cm of water and add the whole garlic clove, lemon slice, bay leaf and a good pinch of salt. Add the artichokes in a single layer and cover the pan. Bring the liquid to the boil over a medium-high heat, then reduce the heat to a simmer. Cover and cook the artichokes until the outer leaves can easily be pulled off, 35–45 minutes.

3. Remove the artichokes from the pan and, once they are cool enough to handle, pull off all the tough outer leaves. Using a spoon, scrape out and discard the inedible fuzzy bit in the centre of the artichoke (it's known as the choke, for good reason: that's what it would make you do if you ate the bloody stuff!). You will be left with artichoke hearts; cut these into 1cm slices.

4. Preheat the oven to 180°C/gas mark 4.

5. Heat the oil in a large frying pan over a medium heat. Add the chopped garlic, followed by the spinach, and cook until the spinach is wilted but still bright green, 2–4 minutes. Remove the pan from the heat and stir in the ricotta cheese and cream cheese, mixing well. Add the sliced artichoke hearts. Stir in the chilli flakes and tahini and season with salt and pepper. Add half of the Parmesan cheese and lemon juice to taste. Mix well.

6. Spread the mixture into a 1-litre baking dish. Sprinkle the remaining Parmesan on top.

7. Bake the dip in the centre of the oven for 15 minutes. Turn on the grill and grill until the cheese has melted and the top is bubbly with lightly browned edges. This will only take a minute or so, so watch carefully and don't bloody burn it. Serve hot, with pitta bread if you like.

LAMB BELLY WITH MINT SAUCE

In the ten years that I've been cooking in the States, I've watched the popularity of lamb grow tremendously. That's a hardship for a lamb lover like me, believe it or not, because it means that prices have gone through the roof for choice bits like chops and roasts. Luckily for me there is plenty of deliciousness to be found in cheap cuts of meat, such as shanks and bellies.

Lamb belly is well marbled with fat and has loads of flavour when cooked correctly. That means rendering – or liquefying – the big strips of fat running through the meat so that you don't end up with a mouthful of solid lard. In this recipe, the lamb belly cooks slowly in a sealed packet, allowing all that lovely fat to render down and baste the meat. You're left with a thin sheet of very tender, almost confit belly meat. We finish it on the grill for a hint of that bitter, smoky flavour of char and serve it with a sweet-and-sour mint sauce, both of which balance out the lovely fattiness.

SERVES 4–6

2 × 450–675g lamb bellies

coarse sea salt and freshly ground black pepper

½ teaspoon chopped fresh thyme

½ teaspoon chopped fresh rosemary

3 tablespoons malt vinegar

1 tablespoon light brown sugar

5 tablespoons chopped fresh mint

1. Preheat the oven to 150°C/gas mark 2.

2. Trim the lamb bellies of excess fat and sinew and season them with salt, pepper and the thyme and rosemary.

3. Pull a piece of clingfilm out onto a clean work surface, press the two lamb bellies together, and roll them in plastic no fewer than 2–3 times, keeping the bellies as flat as possible. Turn the bellies 180 degrees and wrap them in two–three more layers of clingfilm. Now repeat the process using foil.

4. Place the lamb belly parcel in a large roasting tin and pour hot water in to reach halfway up the bellies. Place the roasting tin on the hob and bring the water to the boil over a high heat. Carefully transfer the tin to the oven and cook it for 3 hours, topping up the water as necessary to keep it at around the same level. Remove it from oven and allow it to rest for 1 hour. Unwrap the meat once it's cool enough to handle, or transfer it still wrapped to the fridge, where it will keep for up to 4 days.

5. Meanwhile, place the vinegar and brown sugar in a small pan and warm it over a medium heat, stirring until the sugar dissolves. Remove the pan from the heat and allow it to cool. Stir in the mint and let it marinate.

6. Prepare your grill for medium-high-heat cooking. Grill the lamb bellies for 2–3 minutes per side. Remove them to a serving plate or chopping board, spoon the mint sauce over the top and serve.

CORN ON THE COB WITH CHILLI-LIME BUTTER

As good as simple steamed corn on the cob can be, the roasty, rich, charred flavour you get by cooking it over dry heat is truly unbeatable. The most common way to do this is to put the corn on the grill, but you can follow the same method using a 245°C/gas mark 9 oven instead. Just cook the corn cobs on top of a baking sheet that's been preheated along with the oven.

If the dried milk powder is weirding you out, give me the benefit of the doubt. It adds some cheesy sweetness to balance the hot and sour butter, as well as a little bit of crunchy texture. All in all, the dish is a spin on *elotes*, the grilled corn covered in cheese that's a common Mexican street food.

SERVES 8

115g unsalted butter, at room temperature

1 tinned chipotle chilli in adobo, finely chopped

1 tablespoon freshly grated lime zest

1½ tablespoons coarse sea salt, plus more for seasoning

1½ tablespoons Maldon sea salt or fleur de sel

1½ tablespoons Maldon smoked salt

1 teaspoon hot smoked paprika

1 tablespoon coarsely ground black pepper

5 tablespoons dried milk powder

8 ears sweetcorn, shucked

vegetable oil for drizzling

1. Place the butter on a chopping board and sprinkle it with the chopped chipotle, lime zest and a little coarse sea salt. Using a knife, finely chop the ingredients together until they're well combined. Transfer the butter mixture to a sheet of greaseproof paper, greaseproof paper or clingfilm. Fold the paper over and roll it into a cylinder, twisting the ends. Wrap that airtight in foil, then chill the butter until solid. It will keep refrigerated for up to 2 weeks or frozen for up to 3 months.

2. Fire up your gas or charcoal grill as hot as it will go. Mix together the three salts, paprika and black pepper in a small bowl and set it aside.

3. In a small frying pan over a medium heat, toast off the milk powder until golden brown, 3–5 minutes, tossing it constantly to avoid burning. Set aside.

4. Drizzle the corn cobs with oil, rubbing to coat each ear thoroughly. Place them on the grill's cooking grate, turning them often, until the corn is lightly charred all over and just tender, about 15 minutes. Transfer the corn to a large serving plate and serve it with the lime chipotle butter, seasoned salts and caramelised milk powder on the side. Job done.

LAMBURGERS

What it is it about men and beef? People can't seem to stop themselves from giving chaps recipe upon recipe for hamburgers and steak, even though neither is really all that complicated. I figured that if I was going to show you yet another burger, it ought to be made from lamb.

I love lamb in general and find that it's exceptionally good in burger format. Just ask the Turks; their *doner kebabs* are basically little lamburgers on sticks. The fattiness of minced lamb makes for incredibly juicy burgers, with the kind of flavour you could only get from beef by grinding up a dry-aged porterhouse. I've kitted these out with my favourite toppings – mushrooms, Gruyère cheese, onion marmalade, rocket and a vinegary, hot, minty yogurt sauce that puts Big Mac sauce to shame – but you can top them with whatever you please. Make sure to use a sturdy bun, which can stand up to the profusion of juices that will come from the meat. And of course, if you don't care for lamb, you can always substitute minced beef and make these regular old hamburgers.

SERVES 4

15g unsalted butter

100g sliced white mushrooms

900g minced lamb

sea salt

4 tablespoons Caramelised Onion Compote (page 21)

4 slices Gruyère or other Swiss cheese

4 burger buns

20g rocket leaves

freshly ground black pepper

olive oil for drizzling

4 tablespoons Special Sauce (recipe follows)

1. Heat the butter in a cast-iron pan over a medium-high heat until it melts and begins to foam. Add the mushrooms and cook until soft and golden, 4–5 minutes. Set aside.

2. Prepare your grill for medium-high-heat cooking.

3. Divide your lamb into four 225g portions. Season them generously with salt and roll each into a ball. Wrap the balls tightly in clingfilm and then flatten them with the heel of your hand into patties about 12.5cm in diameter and 1cm thick; the plastic will help mould and pack the meat. Use your thumb to make a dimple in the centre of the patty (this helps the burger keep its shape as it cooks). Remove the clingfilm.

4. Gently place the burgers on the grill over direct heat. Resist the urge to mash them into the grate with a spatula, which does nothing to help them cook nicely. Leave them alone for 3 minutes for medium-rare; add a minute or two for a better-cooked burger. Flip them, and after 2 minutes, top each with the Caramelised Onion Compote, mushrooms and cheese. Cook the burgers for a further minute, then remove them to a serving plate or baking sheet. They should measure 52°C for medium-rare, 57°C for medium.

5. Place the buns on the grill cut-side down for a minute or two to warm them. In a small bowl, dress the rocket with salt, pepper and a bit of oil.

6. Spread the bottom of each bun with Special Sauce, then transfer the burgers to their buns. Top them with the rocket, close with a bun and serve.

(continued)

SPECIAL SAUCE

MAKES 180ML

115g Greek yogurt

1 tablespoon diced roasted red pepper

1 tablespoon diced cornichons

1 tablespoon diced capers

1½ teaspoons fresh lemon juice

1½ teaspoons harissa paste or harissa powder

1 tablespoon chopped fresh mint

1 tablespoon chopped fresh coriander

coarse sea salt and freshly ground black pepper

Chuck all the ingredients in a small bowl, mix them well and season the sauce with salt and pepper.

GIVE IT SOME GAS

Chefs tend to go absolutely mental on the subject of charcoal grilling and its superiority to grilling with propane gas. Charcoal's flavour is the whole point, they'll argue, and there's an art to managing the heat of a live fire. Gas grilling, with its push-button ignition and temperature-altering knobs, is for amateurs.

Call me a sell-out, but while gas grilling may be a little lacking in the romance department, it's also about a thousand times more convenient than mucking about with charcoal on your average weeknight. With a charcoal grill, there is the stacking and lighting of the coals to manage and the wait for them to turn ready for cooking; with gas, you flick a switch and go. Since a charcoal fire burns hot for hours, it would be madness to get the grill going for a single piece of fish; gas, on the other hand, goes off and on instantly. I won't deny that charcoal lends its own delicious flavour to food, but insisting on charcoal is letting the perfect be the enemy of the good.

There's also a common misconception that if you buy a gas grill, it needs to be big and tricked out to do the job right. The truth is, even those little piece of shit grills with portable propane canisters are perfectly all right to use.

There is good reason to make grilling as easy as possible. It's super healthy, since you use no cooking fat and the grilling process actually drains fat away from meats. Cooking directly over a flame, even a gas flame, produces a beautiful chargrilled flavour that isn't easy to achieve in the oven or on the hob. And getting a breath of fresh air while you make dinner is a nice bonus of its own, wouldn't you say?

ROOT VEGETABLES

Root vegetables might not be the first thing that comes to mind when you think about grilling – most people go straight to summer produce like courgettes, aubergines and peppers. But the abundant natural sugars in carrots, parsnips, turnips and the like react beautifully to the dry heat of the grill, caramelising, intensifying and charring.

A note about the oil you use: I call for blended oil here, which you'll see on the grocery shop shelf as a blend of about 75 per cent vegetable oil and 25 per cent olive oil. Try to avoid pure olive oil, which can lend a bitter taste when heated to high temperatures.

SERVES 4–6

2 carrots, peeled and split

2 parsnips, peeled and split

1 celeriac, peeled and cut into 1cm planks

2 small fennel bulbs, split

1 swede, peeled and cut into 1cm planks

1 turnip, peeled and cut into 1cm planks

4 tablespoons blended vegetable oil

coarse sea salt and freshly ground black pepper

115g unsalted butter

zest of 1 lemon

1 tablespoon finely chopped fines herbes (parsley, chives, tarragon and chervil)

1. Prepare the grill for medium-high-heat cooking.

2. In a large bowl, toss all of the vegetables in the oil with a generous sprinkling of salt and a few grinds of pepper.

3. Place the vegetables on the grill, avoiding any hot spots. Grill the vegetables on all sides until cooked through and tender, 7–10 minutes. Remove them from the grill.

4. Place a small saucepan on the grill and melt your butter in it.

5. In a large bowl, toss the grilled vegetables, melted butter, lemon zest and fines herbes. Taste and add salt as needed. Arrange the veg on a big serving plate and serve.

SWORDFISH WITH SALSA VERDE

I had never tried swordfish until I moved to the States, and even then it wasn't until I watched the film *The Perfect Storm* and had to see what all the fuss was about. It turns out that fresh-caught swordfish really is good enough to risk life and limb over. It's meaty in both flavour and texture, so if you're not much of a fish eater, this is a great place to start. You might remember that back in the 90s Atlantic swordfish was being overfished and therefore wasn't a responsible species to eat. Now, thanks to good fishery management, swordfish populations are back on solid footing and it's a perfectly sustainable seafood option.

SERVES 4

4 tablespoons salted capers, soaked for 30 minutes, drained, and roughly chopped

15g fresh flat-leaf parsley, chopped

25g spring onions, white and green parts, chopped

15g fresh mint leaves, chopped

150ml fresh lemon juice

2 teaspoons grated lemon zest

270ml extra virgin olive oil

2 teaspoons crushed chilli flakes

coarse sea salt

1½ teaspoons freshly ground black pepper

4 × 170g swordfish steaks, 2cm thick

1. Chuck the capers, parsley, spring onions, mint, 120ml of the lemon juice, the lemon zest, 240ml oil and 1 teaspoon of the chilli flakes in the jug of a blender. Purée them until smooth, season with salt and pepper and set aside.

2. Prepare the grill for medium-high-heat cooking. Mix together the remaining 2 tablespoons lemon juice and remaining 2 tablespoons oil. Brush the swordfish steaks on both sides with the lemon-oil mixture and season them with salt and the remaining 1 teaspoon chilli flakes.

3. Grill the steaks until just cooked through, 3–4 minutes per side and transfer them to plates. Spoon the salsa verde over the top and serve them with Plain Boiled Potatoes (page 138) and Butterhead Lettuce Salad (page 121).

CHICKEN AL MATTONE

I've had a thing for Italian food since I was a very young boy. My aunt was from Italy, and at her house I was exposed to really good homemade pasta, gnocchi, mortadella and my favourite, Nutella. Her relatives would visit with all sorts of goodies, from salamis to prosciutto to Italian cheeses. It was probably little influences like these that subconsciously drew me to becoming a chef; that and the fact that David Beckham was better at football than me, so I didn't get the call! And of course laying bricks just didn't have the same appeal.

Here is a dish of pure simplicity, using only a few ingredients and a very clever cooking technique – what we call 'chicken under a brick' in Britain and America. Only the bloody Italians could come up with something this easy and tasty.

SERVES 3–4

1 × 1.5–1.8kg
organic chicken

4 tablespoons fresh
lemon juice

3 tablespoons grapeseed
or olive oil

1 tablespoon chopped fresh
rosemary, plus additional
sprigs for garnish

2 garlic cloves, crushed

coarse sea salt and freshly
ground black pepper

¼ teaspoon chilli flakes

chopped fresh flat-
leaf parsley

1. Using a sharp chef's knife or a pair of poultry shears, cut the backbone out of the chicken so that the whole bird can be flattened into a single layer. This technique is called *spatchcock* (save the jokes for later, lads).

2. Place the chicken flat, skin-side down, on a baking sheet. Mix 2 tablespoons of the lemon juice, 2 tablespoons of the oil, the chopped rosemary and garlic in a small bowl. Rub the mixture all over the chicken on both sides. Cover the chicken with clingfilm and bang it in the fridge overnight.

3. Prepare your grill for low-heat cooking (around 120–135°C).

4. Brush the chicken with the remaining tablespoon of cooking oil and sprinkle it with salt and pepper. Put the chicken skin-side down on the grill, away from the flames.

5. Place a foil-wrapped brick (or cast-iron frying pan) on top of the chicken so that it sits perpendicular to the breastbone, keeping the chicken from buckling up. Grill the bird for 45–60 minutes (a general rule of thumb for chicken is about 18–20 minutes per 450g).

6. Remove the brick and turn the chicken over, then put the brick back in place and continue to grill until juices run clear when the thickest part of a thigh is pierced, for a further 10–15 minutes.

7. Remove the brick and transfer the chicken to a plate. Drizzle it with the remaining 2 tablespoons lemon juice and sprinkle it with the chilli flakes, some parsley and rosemary.

GAME DAY

HOMEMADE PITTA BREAD

SPICED LAMB SHANKS

SPICED YOGURT DIP

SWEET CHILLI MARMALADE (PAGE 26)

INFUSED VINEGARS (PAGE 34)

MAYBE THE ESKIMOS ARE AN EXCEPTION, BUT MEN IN EVERY CULTURE, in every country around the world that I'm aware of, have the lads over from time to time to watch a game. In England, that game is football, rugby or cricket, and it usually involves plenty of good, cold lagers and rib-sticking refreshments of some sort – often just chips and dips, but your better hosts will put together something a bit more inspired. For those occasions, here is a simple but delicious menu of fork-tender lamb shanks, homemade pitta bread and the necessary accompaniments – spiced yogurt dip, chilli marmalade and infused vinegars for dipping and dressing these lamb sandwiches. Better than fast-food pizza and wings, wouldn't you say?

HOMEMADE PITTA BREAD

I read somewhere that it was our ability to farm wheat and make bread that changed the course of human history, giving birth to civilisation. That certainly seems logical, as practically every nation and its people have their own form of bread that they make and eat. The pitta comes from the Mediterranean and Middle East, which makes it one of the oldest forms of bread around.

Some breads are very complex to prepare, shape and bake correctly, but pittas are quite rustic and straightforward. For this recipe, you'll need a small stand mixer or large triceps, plus a rolling pin, an oven, a bread stone (preferable) or two baking sheets (less ideal but OK). This recipe uses the 'mother' method, which means that you first make a pre-fermentation starter before making the actual bread (see page 50 for more about bread mothers). It helps the bread rise (or 'proof') well and lends it a really nice flavour profile.

MAKES 16 PITTAS

1 teaspoon dried active yeast

600ml warm water (approximately 40°C)

260g wholemeal flour

about 560g strong bread flour

1 tablespoon sea salt

1–2 tablespoons olive oil

1. In the bowl of a stand mixer fitted with a dough hook attachment, combine the yeast and warm water. Turn the mixer on low speed just to stir the yeast mixture to help it dissolve.

2. Add the wholemeal flour, 130g at a time, followed by 150g of the bread flour. Mix the dough for 2 minutes to activate the gluten in the flour. Turn off the mixer, loosely cover the bowl with clingfilm and let it rest until it doubles in size, about 30 minutes.

3. Sprinkle the dough with salt and stir in the oil. Mix for 2 minutes. Add the remainder of the bread flour, 140g at a time, and knead it with the dough hook on medium speed for 8–10 minutes, until the dough is elastic and pulls away from the bowl as one smooth mass.

4. Lightly oil the surface of the dough and cover it with clingfilm. Let rise until at least double in size, approximately 1 hour 30 minutes.

5. Turn the dough out onto a floured work surface and knock the air out of it with your hands. Portion out 16 eyeball-even balls and roll them out into circles approximately 20–23cm in diameter and less than 6mm thick.

6. Preheat oven to 230°C/gas mark 8 and place a large baking stone or two baking sheets on a rack or racks towards the bottom of the oven.

7. Working in batches, bake the pittas for 5 minutes. Remove them from the oven and place them on a cooling rack for about 5 minutes to cool slightly, then wrap the breads in a large tea towel (this will keep them soft). Stuff and eat them immediately, or reheat them before use either in the oven or on a griddle.

SPICED LAMB SHANKS

I love shank meat of all sorts. It's got a lovely melt-in-your-mouth texture and a strong flavour of whatever beast you're eating, whether it's beef, veal, pork or lamb. But this is a cut that you've got to cook low and slow, or else the meat will be tough as leather. I let these lamb shanks simmer away for hours in wine and stock flavoured with warm spices, and the result is absolutely incredible. If you cook only one recipe from this book, it should be this. Wrapping the meat up in pitta with a bit of yogurt sauce is ambrosia. Enjoy.

SERVES 4

1½ tablespoons olive oil

4 lamb shanks

3 onions, thinly sliced

4 garlic cloves, thinly sliced

½ cinnamon stick

2 star anise

1 tablespoon cumin seeds, crushed

1 tablespoon coriander seeds, crushed

pinch of chilli flakes

500ml red wine

2 × 400g tins chopped tomatoes

115g dates (about 5 dates)

950ml low-sodium beef stock

2 tablespoons pomegranate molasses

sea salt

handful of chopped fresh coriander

1. Preheat the oven to 150°C/gas mark 2.

2. Place a Dutch oven big enough to hold the lamb shanks over a medium-high heat and add the oil. Working in batches so as not to crowd the pan, caramelise the shanks, turning them every couple of minutes so they brown on all surfaces. Remove them from the pan and set them aside.

3. Reduce the heat to medium, add the onions to the pan and cook until soft and translucent, about 10 minutes. Add the garlic and spices and cook for 4 further minutes. Add the wine and reduce it by two thirds, about 15 minutes. Chuck in the tomatoes, dates and stock, then nestle the shanks back in on their sides so that they're mostly submerged in liquid. Bring the liquid to the boil, cover and put it in the oven. Cook for 3–4 hours, until fork-tender.

4. Remove the lid and stir through the molasses. Pull out the shanks and wrap them in foil to keep them warm. Place the Dutch oven over a medium heat, bring the cooking liquid to the simmer, and reduce it down until thick and glossy. Stir it regularly to keep the sauce together.

5. Taste the sauce and add salt as needed. Place the shanks on a big serving plate and pour the sauce over the top. Scatter with coriander and serve. You can pull the meat off the bones, drizzle it with the Spiced Yogurt Dip (page 160) and serve in Pita Bread (page 157).

SPICED YOGURT DIP

When you think 'English chef', your mind probably goes to fish and chips, roast beef and sticky toffee pudding. The truth is, I think the most eaten dish in England for the past twenty years has been chicken tikka masala! We Brits absolutely love Indian food, so it seemed only right to include at least one recipe from the subcontinent in this book. This cooling yogurt sauce is known as *raita* in Indian cuisine, and it's wonderful for taking the edge off spicy or rich foods.

MAKES 675ML

1 cucumber, thinly sliced

coarse sea salt

450–500ml whole milk yogurt (not the Greek variety)

55g red onion, finely chopped

4 tablespoons roughly chopped fresh coriander

2 tablespoons fresh lime juice

¼ teaspoon ground coriander

¼ teaspoon ground cumin

⅛ teaspoon freshly ground black pepper

tiny pinch of freshly grated nutmeg

tiny pinch of ground cinnamon

tiny pinch of ground cardamom

1. Place the cucumber slices in a colander and sprinkle them liberally with salt, tossing to combine. Let the cukes drain for 30 minutes, then rinse them with cold water. Place the cucumbers between paper towels for 5 minutes, pressing down from time to time to extract as much water as possible.

2. In a medium bowl, combine the cucumber slices with the remaining ingredients and season with salt.

CHRISTMAS

A CHRISTMAS PUNCH

CHICKEN LIVER PÂTÉ

A JOINT OF BEEF AND A PROPER GRAVY

TURNIP AND POTATO GRATIN

YORKSHIRE PUDDINGS

EGGNOG ICE CREAM

APPLE PIE

CHRISTMAS IS TYPICALLY A TIME OF YEAR WHEN WIVES AND MUMS ALWAYS have their hands full, and I've found it to be a good opportunity for the men of the family to step up, show their worth and take charge of some of the festive food. It is also, in truth, a fantastic time to be on kitchen duty. Christmas feasting is all about rich and indulgent flavours, without any particular consideration for waistlines or wallets. A word to the wise: having a bowl of punch on the go means you'll have lots of company in the kitchen, which means extra hands for peeling, chopping and mixing.

A CHRISTMAS PUNCH

In England we always drink punch at Christmas, so obviously I got hammered on the stuff when I was about eleven and didn't touch it again until well into my thirties. Now I'm old enough to fully appreciate how gathering around a punch bowl is a perfect fit for the festive, social nature of the holidays. It also frees the host up from mixing individual drinks to better focus on cooking, opening presents and general merrymaking.

SERVES 8–12

peels from 3 lemons (ideally without any white pith)

18 white sugar cubes

18 fresh strawberries, hulled and sliced

3 rounds fresh pineapple, each cut into 8 pieces

1 tablespoon vanilla extract

360ml bourbon whiskey (I like Buffalo Trace)

180ml gin (any London dry will do)

540ml chilled sparkling water

1. In a medium bowl, combine the lemon peels and sugar. Mix them up and mash them with the back of a spoon (this is called *muddling*) to extract their oil. Leave the mixture for at least an hour or up to three hours, taking a crack at muddling the peels and sugar from time to time. Eventually a syrup will form from the sugar and lemon oil.

2. Add the strawberries, pineapple and vanilla. Stir well and let sit for another hour.

3. Add the booze and refrigerate for at least 2 hours.

4. Transfer the liquid to a punch bowl, top it off with the sparkling water, and serve in glasses filled with ice. Don't ice the punch; ice the glasses instead.

CHICKEN LIVER PÂTÉ

This is the perfect gateway project for the budding charcuterie maker, ideal for the holiday season when friends and family are constantly in and out of your house and you're looking for something to give them that's a bit more festive than the same old crisps or Doritos. It's quite easy to make, and the result is so luxurious that you'll wish you had discovered it years ago. If you're feeling flush and have the momentum, then substitute half the chicken livers for the same weight in foie gras. Heavenly!

MAKES FOUR 120ML JARS

45ml ruby port

45ml Madeira

45ml cognac

1 tablespoon finely diced shallot

1 garlic clove

1 bay leaf

1 sprig thyme

250g chicken livers

1 teaspoon coarse sea salt

1 teaspoon pink curing salt (also called Prague powder No.2)

½ teaspoon freshly ground black pepper

2 medium eggs

225g unsalted butter, diced

3½ tablespoons unsalted butter, melted in the microwave

1. In a medium heavy-based saucepan set over a medium heat, combine all the booze plus the shallot, garlic, bay leaf and thyme and bring it to a simmer. Allow to reduce until syrupy, about 10 minutes. Remove from the heat and let cool.

2. Add the livers, coarse sea salt, curing salt and pepper to the wine reduction and place it in a 4-litre ziplock bag. Crack your eggs into a second ziplock bag and place the diced butter into a third bag.

3. Fill a sink or a very large bowl with very warm water and soak the 3 sealed bags until the butter is melted but not separated. This should take about 15 minutes.

4. Sterilise four 120ml mason jars by dunking them in boiling water for 10 minutes; remove them with metal tongs and dry them well. Line a roasting tin with a tea towel and place the mason jars on top.

5. Meanwhile, preheat oven to 100°C/gas mark ¼.

6. Dump the eggs into a blender or food processor and process them for 1 minute. With the blender still running, add the liver mixture and continue blending for a further 1–2 minutes until it's silky smooth. With the blender running, slowly add in your liquid ziplocked butter and process until the butter is fully incorporated. Pass the mousse through a fine-mesh sieve and into a clean bowl.

7. Divide the mixture among the mason jars and cover them individually with clingfilm. Pour hot tap water into the roasting tin to reach halfway up the jars and bake for 30–45 minutes, until they measure 48°C in the centre (how's that for precision?). Remove the clingfilm the second those mousses leave the oven so that water droplets don't have a chance to condense on the surface, and place them in the fridge for about an hour to cool.

8. Top the mousse pots with a layer of melted butter to seal them, then cover them with lids and return them to the fridge. Allow them 24 hours in the fridge to set up nicely before serving. They will live there quite happily for up to 2 weeks.

A JOINT OF BEEF AND A PROPER GRAVY

I've not lived in England for a very long time, but as the saying goes, you can take the man out of the country, but you'll never take the country out of the man. Roast beef and gravy is what a festive meal in England is all about. When I was the executive chef for the Palihouse Hotel in LA, I used to do a bang-up British roast much like this one that attracted all sorts of famous expats, from football players to actors to musicians, each hungering for a taste of home. It was a blast.

SERVES 6

1 × 1.3–1.8kg bone-in rib-eye joint

coarse sea salt and freshly ground black pepper

115g unsalted butter

1 carrot, chopped

1 onion, chopped

2 sticks celery, chopped

1 leek, chopped and thoroughly washed

1 head garlic, cut in half

½ bottle red wine

2 tablespoons plain flour

1.2 litres beef stock

1. Hit the rib-eye joint with plenty of salt on all sides, really seasoning the shit out of it. For the best results, do this 24 hours in advance; this helps the seasoning fully penetrate the roast and dries out the surface so that it sears better.

2. Preheat the oven to 160°C/gas mark 3.

3. Heat a large roasting tin or Dutch oven on the hob over a medium heat and add the butter. Allow it to melt and go nut brown and foamy. Place the beef in the tin fat-side down and let it sear for 5–7 minutes, until golden brown (always start with the fat-side down, as you want to render away that fat and utilise it for searing the rest of the meat). Repeat the searing on all sides of the beef. Remove the joint to a plate and set it aside.

4. Add the carrot, onion, celery and leek to the tin and sweat them down in the fat for 3 minutes, or until the onions are translucent. Mound up the veg, and garlic and put the beef back on top. Chuck it in the oven, uncovered, for 15–18 minutes per 450g – so about 1 hour for a roast of this size. You're looking for an internal temperature of 52°C for medium-rare and 54°C–57°C for medium.

5. While the beef cooks, pour the wine into a medium saucepan over a high heat and reduce it down by two thirds, about 15 minutes. Set aside.

6. Remove the beef from the oven, transfer it to a chopping board, and tent it with foil to keep the heat and moisture in. Set your roasting tin on the hob over medium heat and stir the flour into the pan drippings. Cook, stirring, for 5–7 minutes, until it begins to brown. Whisk in the wine in a slow stream, followed by the beef stock. Bring the liquid to the simmer and cook uncovered for 10–15 minutes to reduce the volume slightly.

7. Strain the gravy into a jug. Slice the beef, working against the grain, and serve with your favourite vegetables and Yorkshire Puddings (page 168).

POTATO AND TURNIP GRATIN

Potato gratin is a classic dish for good reason; there's little on earth that compares to the trio of potatoes, cream and cheese. If I'm honest, I started adding in turnips to begin with because one of my sous-chefs over-ordered them and we had loads in the fridge to get rid of. But we stumbled onto something truly wonderful, with the sweetness of the turnips balancing out the saltiness of Parmesan cheese. Now I wouldn't do gratin any other way.

SERVES 6

15g unsalted butter

2 medium to large turnips

900g peeled Maris Piper potatoes about 4 large potatoes)

500ml double cream

2 shall ts, finely diced

170g grated Parmesan

1 teaspoon sea salt

½ teaspoon freshly ground black pepper

1. Preheat the oven to 160°C/gas mark 3.

2. Butter the inside of a 25cm × 38cm Pyrex or ceramic baking dish. Slice the turnips razor thin, about 1.5mm, using a very sharp knife or, ideally, a mandoline slicer (watch your fingers, lads; Christmas is a bad time to head to the hospital). Follow with the potatoes.

3. In a medium bowl, mix the sliced turnips with half the cream, half the shallots, 65g of the Parmesan and half the salt and pepper. Repeat in a second bowl with the potatoes.

4. Now we start layering, which is a bit of a swine, but it's necessary. First lay down a single layer of potatoes, followed by a single layer of turnips, and so on and so forth until you run out of both. Pour any excess cream left in the bowls over the top of the gratin. Sprinkle the remaining Parmesan over the top.

5. Chuck the gratin in the oven and bake until fork-tender and golden brown, 30–45 minutes. Allow it to cool off for 10 minutes before eating, as it will be incredibly hot and would otherwise burn the shit out of your mouth.

YORKSHIRE PUDDINGS

My Sunday in England was a family day. Growing up, we'd watch a football match, do some chores (which, of course, I hated), and then a big cooked lunch usually started around 3 or 4 o'clock. This was the main meal of the day on Sundays and we always sat down to it as a family, sometimes with cousins and aunts and uncles added into the mix. There would be three or four types of vegetables, potatoes, gravy and a roast of some sort: beef with horseradish cream, chicken with sage and onion stuffing, lamb with mint sauce or pork with applesauce. And there were always Yorkshire puddings, baked golden and puffy. My mother would have to make extra to fill with lemon curd and vanilla so that we kids could eat them for dessert too.

SERVES 6

3 medium organic eggs

65g plain flour

pinch of sea salt

240ml whole milk

180ml vegetable oil

1. Whisk the eggs together in a medium bowl until pale and fluffy, about 4 minutes. Add the flour, salt and milk and whisk again until really well incorporated. Pour the batter into a pitcher and let it sit for 30 minutes before you use it.

2. Preheat the oven to 190°C/gas mark 5, preferably on the convection setting if you have it (this circulates the air so that the oven temperature stays even throughout). Place a 12-cup muffin tin in the oven to heat up for 5 minutes. Pour 1 tablespoon oil into each cup, put the tin back into the oven, and heat until the oil is very hot and smoking.

3. Dead gently open the oven door, slide the tin halfway out, and carefully pour the batter into the muffin cups to fill them about halfway. You have to be as quick as you can here, otherwise the oil will cool and the puddings will stick, which is obviously not what you want.

4. Close the oven door and cook the Yorkshire puddings for 15 minutes without opening it. You can peek if you want, but it's better to just be patient. Serve them immediately.

EGGNOG ICE CREAM

This eggnog ice cream is delicious on its own, but especially on top of apple pie.

MAKES 1 LITRE

500ml double cream

240ml whole milk

pinch of sea salt

½ vanilla pod, split open and seeds scraped out

200g granulated sugar

9 medium egg yolks

½ teaspoon freshly grated nutmeg

6 tablespoons dark rum

1. In a heavy-based saucepan over a medium heat, combine the cream, milk, salt and vanilla seeds and bring the mixture to the boil.

2. Meanwhile, in a stand mixer fitted with the whisk attachment, combine the sugar and egg yolks and whisk at medium-high speed until the mixture triples in volume and turns pale yellow, light and creamy. With the mixer running on medium speed, slowly add the hot cream mixture and continue to process until the liquid reaches room temperature. Stir in the nutmeg and rum and chill the ice cream base in the fridge overnight.

3. Churn the base in an ice cream maker according to the manufacturer's instructions.

APPLE PIE

They say in the States that there's nothing more American than apple pie, but I think you can actually thank Great Britain for that one (you're welcome!). We love our apples in the United Kingdom and have hundreds of different varieties, which give us fantastic ciders, preserves, tarts and, yes, pies. This simple recipe is incredible with a scoop of eggnog ice cream – now there's a flavour the Yanks can take credit for through and through.

SERVES 8

260g plain flour

1¼ teaspoons salt

150g solid vegetable fat, plus extra for greasing

4–6 tablespoons cold water

600g Pink Lady or Granny Smith apples, peeled and sliced

4 tablespoons brown sugar

100g granulated sugar

1 teaspoon ground cinnamon

⅛ teaspoon freshly grated nutmeg

⅛ teaspoon ground allspice

1 tablespoon fresh lemon juice

2 tablespoons cornflour

simple syrup (optional)

demerara sugar (optional)

1. Combine the flour, 1 teaspoon of the salt and the vegetable fat in a food processor and pulse to blend them together until you have pea-size flakes. Slowly add the cold water 1 tablespoon at a time until the dough is moist and begins to pull away slightly from the walls of the food processor.

2. Divide the dough into two equal balls. Lightly flour them and flatten them into discs. Wrap each tightly in clingfilm and refrigerate them for at least 45 minutes and up to 24 hours.

3. Preheat the oven to 220°C/gas mark 7.

4. Remove the dough from the fridge and grease a pie tin with a bit of vegetable fat or cooking spray. On a lightly floured work surface, roll out one piece of dough into a round slightly larger than the circumference of the upside-down pie tin. Carefully roll the dough around a floured rolling pin; gently unfurl it across the top of the pie tin. Roll a small dough scrap into a little ball, dust it with floor, and use it to gently press the dough into the pie tin (using your warm fingers will often break the dough).

5. In a large bowl, combine the apples, brown sugar, granulated sugar, spices, lemon juice, cornflour and remaining ¼ teaspoon salt and mix them well. Scrape them into the pie tin.

6. On a lightly floured work surface, roll out your second piece of dough. Carefully roll the dough around a floured rolling pin; gently unfurl it across the top of the pie tin. Crimp the edges of the crust together with your fingers or a fork to seal the dough. Remove any excess dough with a sharp knife and cut a couple of slits in the centre for steam to escape. Place the pie tin on a baking sheet.

7. Bake the pie for 40–50 minutes, until deep golden brown. If you'd like, halfway through baking you can brush the top of the pie with a bit of simple syrup and sprinkle it with large grains of demerara sugar. Remove the pie from the oven and let it set for at least 2 hours before serving.

PUDDING

IF YOU'RE SCRATCHING YOUR HEAD AND WONDERING WHY I'VE DEVOTED AN ENTIRE chapter to puddings, you can relax: unlike the US where 'pudding' refers to a particular type of dessert, in the UK it encompasses the whole gamut of cakes, tarts, pies, ice cream, cookies, crumbles and cobblers. Puddings, all.

I have a real fondness for baking, more so I think than the average chef. I like the creative aspect of pastry work and the chemistry at play in baking. It's much more technical than savoury cooking and tends to require more precision. I might have become a pastry chef, only my hands are always too hot! Which is a disaster when you're working with delicate doughs all day long.

My taste in dessert runs towards the traditional. I'm not a big fan of savoury flavours or complicated presentations. I think that a good meal should end with something sweet and comforting. What follows are my most tried-and-true recipes for pudding.

STICKY TOFFEE PUDDING

We English have a horrific sweet tooth, and sate it with all manner of rich, sugary cakes, trifles and soft, gooey puddings (as well as awesome sweets, by the way – I have yet to find anything in America that rivals a Cadbury Flake). Sticky toffee pudding is one of our best, and probably the most famous outside England. I have made this recipe more times than I can count and number it among my favourites.

There's not much to it aside from mixing the batter as little as possible. The more air you whisk into the eggs and baking powder, the more the mixture will rise in the oven, and a pudding like this one is meant to be dense enough to put you into a good food coma for two to three hours.

SERVES 4

55g unsalted butter,
plus extra for greasing

500ml double cream

100ml muscovado sugar

2½ teaspoons golden
syrup or molasses

fine sea salt

8–10 pitted Medjool dates

1 teaspoon bicarbonate
of soda

175g plain flour

1 teaspoon baking powder

150g granulated sugar

4 medium eggs

1 teaspoon vanilla extract

1 tablespoon brewed
espresso

1 teaspoon black treacle

whipped cream, ice cream
or crème fraîche, to serve

1. Preheat the oven to 180°C/gas mark 4 and butter a 22cm porcelain soufflé dish (or a baking dish of a similar size).

2. Knock together the toffee sauce by bringing the cream, muscovado sugar, golden syrup and a pinch of salt to the boil in a medium saucepan over a medium-high heat, stirring often to melt the sugar. Reduce the heat and simmer, stirring constantly, for about 5 minutes, until the mixture is thick and coats the back of your spoon. Pour half of the sauce into the prepared soufflé dish and place the dish in the freezer. Set aside the other half.

3. Now to the pudding. Heat the dates and 240ml of water in a medium saucepan set over a medium-high heat. Once the water begins to boil, remove the pan from the heat and stir in the bicarbonate of soda. Set the pan aside someplace where you can keep it slightly warm.

4. Grab a medium bowl and sift together the flour, baking powder and ½ teaspoon salt.

5. In the bowl of a stand mixer fitted with the paddle attachment (hopefully – or you can do this by hand), beat the butter and granulated sugar until light and fluffy. Gradually beat in the eggs, then the vanilla extract, followed by the espresso and black treacle. It's going to look sort of curdled, but that's normal. Stir in half of the flour mixture, then the dates and water, then add the remaining flour mixture until just barely mixed. Don't overbeat the batter or it will raise up like a fifteenth-century Scottish rebel group when you cook it.

6. Remove the soufflé dish from the freezer and scrape in the batter. Bake for 50 minutes, or until a toothpick inserted into the centre of the pudding comes out with moist crumbs attached.

7. Spoon portions of the cake into serving bowls and douse it with your reserved warm toffee sauce. Serve with whipped cream, ice cream or crème fraîche – whatever takes your fancy.

CHOCOLATE MARQUISE WITH CARAMELISED BANANAS

English people take their chocolate very seriously. I absolutely love Cadbury brand, which is nothing fancy but truly delicious. Ever since I was a kid I could eat unhealthy amounts in a single sitting. I have to admit that Cadbury is better suited to eating than cooking, though – for cooking, I use either Valrhona or Cacao Barry (known as Callebaut in the UK) brands in my restaurant, and these are the chocolates I would recommend to you.

Another particular sweet tooth addiction for me is bananas, one of Mother Nature's ready-made desserts. I have fond memories of going to the Mansfield open market with my mum and hearing the local greengrocer shouting out his bounty ('Come get your bananas, 25p a pound! Come on, love, you know you want a banana . . .').

For me, it makes complete sense to bring together two of my favourite ingredients in one dessert. Have your insulin ready for the glycerine shock that's about to hit you, because it is seriously sweet and rich!

SERVES 6–8

1 × 400g tin sweetened condensed milk

450g high-quality milk chocolate, chopped

55g unsalted butter, cut into pieces

240ml cold double cream

200g granulated sugar

½ vanilla pod

2–3 bananas

500ml chocolate chip or dulce de leche ice cream (optional)

dulce de leche sauce (recipe follows)

1. Make the dulce de leche: bring a medium pan of water to the boil and insert the unopened tin of condensed milk. Let it boil for 4 hours, making sure to top up the water whenever necessary so that the pan doesn't boil dry (alternately, 45 minutes in a pressure cooker will do the job). Remove the tin from the heat and let it cool before opening; inside, the milk should be thick and caramel coloured.

2. Lightly oil a 450g loaf tin (about 21 × 10cm), line it with clingfilm and set it aside.

3. In the top of a double boiler or in a metal bowl set over a pan of simmering water, combine the chocolate and butter and melt until smooth, stirring occasionally. Remove from the heat and allow to cool.

4. In the bowl of a stand mixer fitted with the whisk attachment, beat the cream with 2 tablespoons of the dulce de leche and 100g of the sugar. Slit open the vanilla pod and scrape the seeds into the mixture. Whip on medium speed until stiff peaks form. Whisk about one third of the cream into the cooled chocolate, then gently fold in the remaining whipped cream. Pour the chocolate mixture into the prepared tin, smoothing the top with a rubber spatula. Cover with clingfilm and chill it overnight.

5. Unwrap the marquise, invert it onto a serving plate and shake gently to release. Remove the clingfilm from the top and let sit at room temperature for about 15 minutes to soften.

6. Meanwhile, peel and cut the bananas lengthways and sprinkle the remaining 100g sugar liberally but evenly along the flat side of each banana half. Using a butane kitchen torch, flame the bananas until golden and caramelised (the dish is sweet, so a bit of burnt sugar won't hurt – if you go a fraction *Pulp Fiction* on it, don't worry, it'll still be delicious). If you don't have a torch, you can also pop the bananas under a grill set on high.

7. Slice the marquise into 2–2.5cm-thick pieces and divide them among dessert plates. Top each slice with a piece of banana and a scoop of ice cream, if you wish, then drizzle the whole thing with dulce de leche sauce.

DULCE DE LECHE SAUCE

MAKES 360ML

240ml double cream

4 heaped tablespoons Dulce de Leche (page 176)

2 teaspoons rum

In the bowl of a stand mixer fitted with the whisk attachment, gently whip together the cream, dulce de leche and rum until the mixture begins to thicken and coats the back of a spoon. Refrigerate until ready to use.

LEMON TART

My grandma is not a great cook. She's almost one hundred years old as I write this recipe, which means she was born bang in the middle of World War I and was just entering adulthood during World War II – no time to worry about kitchen skills with a war effort on! She was always a career woman, working into her seventies and only taking time off to have her three children. But she did know how to bake a little bit, and would make cakes and biscuits, my favourite jam and lemon tarts.

Now before anyone gets excited that this recipe might be a family heirloom, it most certainly is not. Grandma's was made using shop-bought lemon curd and a pastry made from lard. It did, however, give me an early appreciation for the dessert, so when I moved to the big smoke (aka London) I genuinely thought I was a lemon curd expert. Then I ate a lemon tart at Marco Pierre White's Criterion Brasserie, and it was one of those moments in life when you realise you don't know shit and you have to start at square one.

This isn't Marco's recipe either; his takes incredible skill to cook correctly. But this is a very good lemon tart, in some respects equal to his, just a lot easier for the home cook to master.

SERVES 8

170g cold unsalted butter

400g granulated sugar

½ teaspoon vanilla extract

230g plain flour, plus extra for dusting

¼ teaspoon salt

350g raw rice or pie weights

4 lemons, at room temperature

115g unsalted butter, at room temperature

4 large eggs, at room temperature

1. In the bowl of a stand mixer fitted with the paddle attachment, mix together the cold butter and 100g of the sugar until they are just combined. Add the vanilla extract.

2. In a medium bowl, sift together the flour and ⅛ teaspoon of the salt, then add them to the butter and sugar mixture. Mix on low speed just until the dough comes together. Dump it out onto a flour-dusted surface and shape the dough into a flat disk. Wrap it in clingfilm and refrigerate for 20 minutes.

3. On a flour-dusted work surface, roll the dough into an 28cm round. Curl it around your rolling pin and unfurl it on top of a removable-based tart tin 25cm in diameter. With cold hands so as not to melt the butter, gently press the dough into the pan, slicing any excess off the edges. Chuck the tart shell back in the fridge for 20 minutes to rest; this keeps it from shrinking when baked.

4. Preheat the oven to 180°C/gas mark 4.

5. Lay four sheets of microwave-safe clingfilm over the top of the tart shell and fill it with the rice or pie weights. Bake for 20–25 minutes, until the dough begins to lightly brown. Lift out the weights and bake for 20–25 minutes more, until golden brown. Remove the tart shell from the oven and leave it on the counter to cool.

6. Using a Microplane, zest the lemons into a small bowl, being careful to avoid the white pith. Squeeze the lemons to yield 120ml juice.

7. In the bowl of a stand mixer fitted with the paddle attachment, cream the

(continued)

room-temperature butter, the remaining 300g sugar and the lemon zest until pale and fluffy; this will take 5–6 minutes, scraping the bowl down with a spatula from time to time.

8. Add the eggs one at a time, then add the lemon juice and the remaining ⅛ teaspoon salt. Mix until combined.

9. Pour the lemon curd into a 2-litre saucepan and cook it over a low heat, stirring constantly with a rubber spatula, until thickened, about 10 minutes (the lemon curd will thicken when it reaches about 79°C, or just below a simmer). Remove it from the heat.

10. Fill the tart shell with warm lemon curd and allow it to set at room temperature. Once cooled to room temperature, the tart can be chilled in the refrigerator.

CREPES SUZETTE

With the way that food is going these days, it seems like everyone is outmanoeuvring each other to come up with the edgiest and most original dessert. Me? I like my sweets classic and delicious – full stop. Crepes Suzette is an example of an elegant French recipe that has stood the test of time. When I was young and before my parents decided they didn't like each other anymore, my family did a very typical English thing and stuffed ourselves into a caravan like sardines and drove to France. It's not a great way to travel (come to think of it, maybe that's why they didn't like each other so much!), but once we got there it was brilliant. La Rochelle, a beautiful town in the south of France, was our usual destination. These trips were my first experience eating proper crepes, and they taught me how you can make the most extraordinary and unforgettable food using just a few simple flavours.

Assuming you don't have a crepe pan (and honestly, your average household does not need a crepe pan), go with something made from Teflon. There is no margin of error when cooking paper-thin crepes, so you need a surface that's entirely non-stick.

SERVES 4–6

130g plain flour
120ml whole milk
105ml water
2 medium eggs
about 450g unsalted butter
50g granulated sugar
1½ teaspoons orange zest
120ml freshly squeezed orange juice
120ml Grand Marnier
¼ teaspoon salt
500ml vanilla ice cream
segments from 4–6 oranges

1. Whisk together the flour, milk, water, eggs and 2 tablespoons melted butter until you have a completely smooth batter. Now stick it in the fridge to rest for at least 20 minutes or up to 24 hours (the longer, the better).

2. Melt about 1 tablespoon butter in a crepe pan or 23cm Teflon frying pan over a medium-low heat. Add 3 tablespoons of batter to the pan and swirl until the bottom of the pan is covered with batter. Cook the crepe for 1 minute, or until slightly moist on top and golden underneath.

3. Loosen the edges of the crepe, slide the spatula under it, then gently flip it upside down in the pan. Cook for 1 minute and transfer the crepe to a plate to keep warm. Repeat the process with the remaining batter, buttering the pan again before each addition.

4. Melt 225g of butter in a large frying pan over a medium heat. Stir in the sugar, orange zest, orange juice, Grand Marnier and salt. Let it continue to bubble away until the sauce thickens and the bubbles begin to slow, about 5 minutes. Dip a spoon into the sauce and run your finger across the back; if your finger leaves a trail through the sauce, it's ready.

5. Very delicately lay a crepe flat in the pan, coating one side with sauce. Fold it in quarters and transfer it to a plate. Repeat with the remaining crepes, arranging them 3 per plate. Add a scoop of ice cream and a drizzle of extra sauce over the top. Garnish with orange segments.

BRIOCHE DOUGHNUTS WITH BOURBON GLAZE

In my first couple of years out of culinary school, I worked as a commis at Café Royal on Piccadilly Circus, just as a Dunkin' Donuts was going in a few doors down. I had never had a doughnut before – they are very much an American import – but I quickly learned that doughnuts are something of a perfect food when you are young, broke and working weird hours. I liked them so much that I set to work designing a version that would fit into a restaurant context. This recipe was on the menu at Waterloo & City for most of the time that restaurant was in business due to its tremendous appeal with our diners. It is seriously decadent. Brioche is buttery and rich to begin with, before you go dunking it in hot oil and finishing it with a buttery bourbon glaze.

MAKES 12–18

150ml cold whole milk

2 tablespoons dried active yeast

450g plain flour, plus extra for dusting

50g granulated sugar

2 teaspoons salt

2 medium cold eggs

5 medium cold egg yolks

280g cold butter, cubed

cooking oil

Bourbon Glaze (recipe follows)

1. Place half of the milk in a small bowl and warm it in the microwave until lukewarm. Stir in the yeast and leave it for 3–4 minutes to dissolve.

2. In the bowl of a stand mixer fitted with the paddle attachment, mix the flour, sugar and salt well. Slowly add the eggs and yolks, then scrape the bowl down. Add the remaining (cold) milk and mix well. Add the yeast mixture.

3. With the mixer on medium-high speed, slowly add the butter a few cubes at a time, allowing it to become mostly incorporated before adding more.

4. Line a baking sheet with greaseproof paper and spray it with cooking spray. Transfer the dough to the prepared sheet, cover it with clingfilm and let it rest in the fridge overnight.

5. On a floured work surface, roll out the dough to about 1cm thick. Using a floured biscuit cutter, cut the dough into rounds 2.5–4cm in diameter. Let the doughnuts sit in a warm room until doubled in size, 8–10 minutes.

6. If you've got an electric fryer by chance, use it, because they're way safer; if not, take a heavy pan like a Dutch oven and fill it two thirds full with cooking oil. Position a thermometer in the oil and heat it nice and slow over a medium heat until the temperature reads 180°F. Working a few at a time (don't crowd the pan, gents), fry the doughnuts until golden brown, about 2 minutes per side. Remove from the fryer with a slotted spoon to a kitchen paper-lined baking sheet. Toss each doughnut in bourbon glaze while still warm, or serve the glaze on the side. Eat immediately.

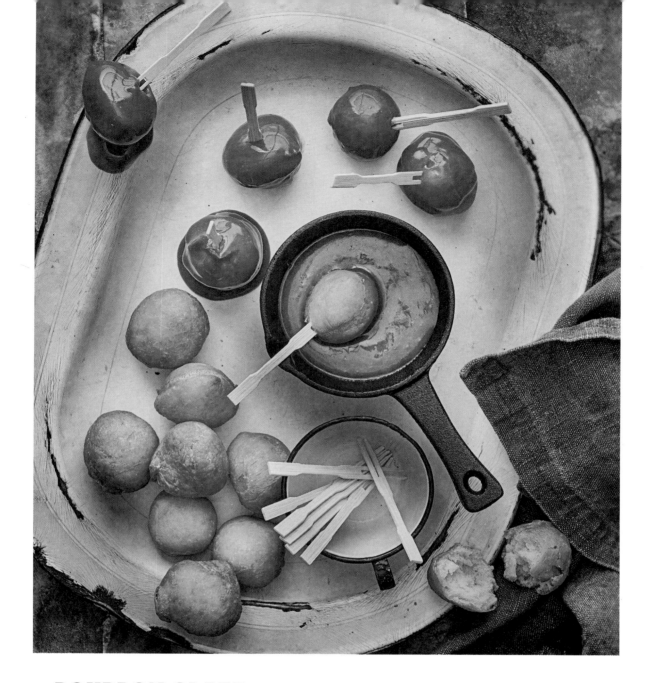

BOURBON GLAZE

MAKES ABOUT 600ML

200g muscovado sugar

seeds from ¼ vanilla pod

1½ teaspoons light corn syrup *or* golden syrup

300g sweetened condensed milk

115g unsalted butter, diced

1 tablespoon bourbon whiskey

1. In a medium saucepan over a medium-high heat, combine the muscovado sugar, vanilla seeds and corn syrup and bring the mixture to the boil, whisking constantly.

2. Once the muscovado sugar is fully melted, reduce the mixture to a simmer and add the condensed milk, butter and bourbon. Continue to simmer, stirring, until all the butter is incorporated and the glaze is smooth.

ETON MESS

For a small island, England has always had plenty of social divides: upper class vs. working class, northerners vs. southerners, EastEnders vs. Coronation Street, your football team vs. his football team, you name it and the English will bicker over it.

This lovely dessert of strawberries, cream and meringue is known in the south of England (and now, around the world) as Eton Mess, named after a very posh school that Prince William attended. Up north where I come from, we just call it strawberries, cream and meringue, because we're not posh and weren't born toffee-nosed with silver spoons wedged up our arses!

Whatever you call it, it is an absolute stunner when the strawberries are fresh and local and relatively easy to put together (you can even use shop-bought meringue to speed up the process if you like). As a kid, we used to make this dessert with the wild strawberries growing in my auntie's garden, and it was simply divine.

SERVES 4

450g strawberries, hulled and roughly chopped

3 tablespoons granulated sugar

240ml double cream

35g icing sugar

1 meringue (recipe follows), smashed up into bite-size pieces

500ml vanilla ice cream

1. Mix together the strawberries and granulated sugar in a large bowl, cover it with clingfilm, and let it sit for 30 minutes to draw the strawberry juices out. Strain the strawberries, reserving the juice.

2. Whisk together the cream and icing sugar in a large bowl until soft peaks form. Gently fold the meringue pieces and berries into the whipped cream.

3. Place some of the strawberry, cream and meringue mixture in the bottom of your bowls. Add a scoop of vanilla ice cream, then top with more mess, drizzle with the reserved strawberry juice for a wonderful sauce and eat your heart out.

MERINGUE

YIELDS 1 LARGE MERINGUE

3 medium egg whites
¼ teaspoon cream of tartar
150g caster sugar
¼ teaspoon vanilla extract

1. Preheat the oven to 100°C/gas mark ¼. Line a baking sheet with greaseproof paper, and if you've got some, hit it with non-stick cooking spray too just in case.

2. In the bowl of an electric stand mixer fitted with the whisk attachment, whisk the egg whites on medium-low speed until foamy. Add the cream of tartar and continue to whisk the whites until they hold soft peaks.

3. Add the sugar a little at a time and continue to whisk, on medium-high speed, until the meringue holds very stiff peaks. Add the vanilla extract. The meringue is done when it holds stiff peaks and when you rub a little between your thumb and index finger it does not feel sandy. If it feels gritty, the sugar has not fully melted, so keep going.

4. Spread the meringue onto your baking sheet about 2cm thick and as evenly as possible. Bake for 1 hour 30 minutes–1 hour 45 minutes, turning the baking sheet halfway through to make sure it bakes evenly. The meringue is done when it is pure white and fairly crisp.

5. Turn off the oven, open the door a crack, and leave the meringue in the oven to finish drying out for an hour or two (or as long as overnight). Store it in an airtight container.

CHOCOLATE AND CARAMEL TRIFLE WITH THE NOSTALGIA OF TWIX

As I've said before, I think the best desserts are the simple and satisfying ones, and a Twix and a glass of milk is one of my all-time favourite vices. Several years back I got to thinking about how I could combine those fabulous flavours of chocolate, caramel and biscuit into a more modern, restaurant-ready dessert. I knew right off the bat that I would do the chocolate component in silky, smooth *panna cotta* form, and shortbread was the obvious stand-in for Twix's crispy biscuit base. But straight caramel would turn out way too sickly sweet in the kind of portion size we were looking at doing. Since Twix and a glass of milk make such a good pairing, I thought why not work the milk right into the dessert with a creamy dulce de leche caramel? And there you have it: my take on Twix.

SERVES 8

THE SHORTBREAD
450g unsalted butter
140g icing sugar
¾ teaspoon salt
seeds from 1 vanilla pod
500g plain flour, plus
extra for dusting

DULCE DE LECHE CREAM
1⅛ teaspoons
powdered gelatine
10 medium egg yolks
450g dulce de leche
(caramel) (see note)
10 medium egg whites

CHOCOLATE PANNA COTTA
2½ teaspoons
powdered gelatine
480ml double cream
480ml whole milk
100g granulated sugar
225g dark chocolate

1. Make the shortbread: in a stand mixer fitted with the paddle attachment, cream together the butter, icing sugar, salt and vanilla seeds. Add the flour and mix until just incorporated.

2. Flatten the dough into a disk, wrap it in clingfilm, and refrigerate it for at least 1 hour or up to 24 hours.

3. Preheat the oven to 180°C/gas mark 4.

4. On a floured work surface, roll out the shortbread to about 6mm thick. Transfer it to a baking sheet lined with greaseproof paper and bake until golden brown, 10–12 minutes. Set aside.

5. Make the dulce de leche cream: in a small bowl, sprinkle the gelatine over 2 tablespoons of room temperature water. Set it aside to bloom while you work.

6. In a stand mixer fitted with the whisk attachment, whisk together the egg yolks and three quarters of the dulce de leche until the mixture doubles in volume, 5–7 minutes. Scrape it into a large bowl and set aside.

7. Whisk the egg whites in the mixer in a clean bowl until they form stiffish peaks. Scrape them into a separate bowl and set them aside.

8. In a small saucepan set over a medium heat, warm the remaining dulce de leche until not quite simmering. Whisk in the gelatine. Remove the mixture from the heat and slowly whisk it into the egg yolk mixture; be careful not to combine the two too quickly, or the heat will cause the yolks to curdle and you'll have a proper mess on your hands. Fold in the egg whites and set aside.

9. Make the chocolate panna cotta: in a small bowl, sprinkle the gelatine over 60ml of room temperature water. Set it aside to bloom while you work.

10. In a medium saucepan set over a medium-high heat, combine the cream, milk and sugar and bring to the boil. Break the chocolate into small chunks and place it in a large bowl.

11. Pour the boiling cream over the top and let it sit for a minute or two to melt the chocolate. Whisk until completely incorporated and let it cool slightly. Whisk in the gelatine. Let cool to room temperature, then refrigerate.

12. To build the dessert: Break the shortbread into even-size chunks, reserving the shortbread crumbs, and use half of them to line the bottom of a 20 × 25 × 5cm Pyrex dish in an even layer. Cover that with the dulce de leche cream. Repeat with another layer of shortbread and refrigerate for at least 1 hour. Top with the chocolate panna cotta, then sprinkle the top with your shortbread crumbs. Allow to set in the fridge overnight.

Note: If you fancy making your own Dulce de Leche, see page 176 for instructions.

INDEX

THANK YOU

- to Kyle Cathie for trusting in me and helping me publish this book

- to Liz Gunnison Dunn for putting up with my busy schedule while writing this book

- to Jessica Goodman, my editor, who occasionally had to jump up and down to get my attention, but it was all worth it

- to everybody who took part in creating this book, including Sharon Bowers, Joh Morris, Judith Hannam, Claire Rogers, Jean Cazals, Alison Lew, Curtis Stone and Jon Taffer

- to Sybil and Harry, my grandparents, for putting me through cooking school

- to Eden and Saffy who stand with me through thick and thin

- to all the employees who worked for me and put up with my bullshit

This book is dedicated to Saffron Rose Collins, who makes everything better. Love, Daddy

First published in Great Britain in 2016 by
Kyle Books, an imprint of Kyle Cathie Ltd
192–198 Vauxhall Bridge Road
London SW1V 1DX
general.enquiries@kylebooks.com
www.kylebooks.co.uk

10 9 8 7 6 5 4 3 2 1

ISBN 978-0-85783-337-2

Project Editor: Jessica Goodman
Copy Editor: Leda Scheintaub
Designer: Alison Lew, Vertigo Design NYC
Photographer: Jean Cazals
Food Stylist: Marie-Ange Lapierre
Prop Stylist: Tamzin Ferdinando
Production: Nic Jones, Gemma John and Lisa Pinnell
Angliciser: Lee Faber
Library of Congress Control Number: 2015953140

Colour reproduction by ALTA London
Printed and bound in China by 1010 International Printing Ltd.